June 7, 2023

For my Dad

Jimmy

Enjoy!

Peter

The

1998
YANKEES

The
1998
YANKEES

THE INSIDE STORY OF THE
GREATEST BASEBALL TEAM EVER

JACK CURRY

12
TWELVE
NEW YORK BOSTON

Twelve
Hachette Book Group
1290 Avenue of the Americas, New York, NY 10104
twelvebooks.com
twitter.com/twelvebooks

First Edition: May 2023

Twelve is an imprint of Grand Central Publishing. The Twelve name and logo are trademarks of Hachette Book Group, Inc.

The publisher is not responsible for websites (or their content) that are not owned by the publisher.

The Hachette Speakers Bureau provides a wide range of authors for speaking events. To find out more, go to hachettespeakersbureau.com or email HachetteSpeakers@hbgusa.com.

Twelve books may be purchased in bulk for business, educational, or promotional use. For information, please contact your local bookseller or the Hachette Book Group Special Markets Department at special.markets@hbgusa.com.

Library of Congress Control Number: 2022952332

ISBNs: 9781538722978 (hardcover), 9781538722992 (ebook)

Printed in the United States of America

LSC-C

Printing 1, 2023

For my dad, Jack: *I hope I have half of your curiosity, your wit, and your street smarts. I know you would have placed this book beside your "Jack's Writing" scrapbook. Proud to be your namesake.*

For my father-in-law, Jack Orbine: *I'm in awe of your vitality, your strength, and your positive attitude. We're forever bonded by your devotion to family and your knowledge of the nuances of baseball.*

The
1998
YANKEES

We were talking about the 1998 Yankees and my question to Derek Jeter was as obvious and as predictable as a question could be. When Jeter reflects upon the 1998 team, that immensely powerful and wonderfully cohesive team, what is the first thing that leaps into his brain?

"Greatest team ever," Jeter said. "That's what comes to mind."

For someone who spent a 20-year career in New York being intentionally bland and not bragging about himself or his teams, Jeter's words were noteworthy and blunt. There were numerous ways Jeter could have praised the 1998 Yankees before instantly describing them as better than any team in baseball history.

He could have gushed about a relentless lineup that drained and destroyed pitchers. He could have raved about a bullish starting rotation that basically featured an ace a day. He could have complimented a balanced bullpen that was anchored by the brilliant Mariano Rivera. Or Jeter could have talked about the unprecedented 125 wins and a season of dominance. But Jeter started at the top. He gave the headline before he discussed the details of the story.

"Hey, look, it's so difficult," Jeter said. "You can't compare eras. It's impossible to do that. The game has changed so much. Look how the game has changed since I retired and that's a short period of time. It's very difficult to compare eras."

Still, even after Jeter hedged a bit in describing how difficult it is to compare teams from different eras, he returned to his original statement. Greatest Team Ever.

"So, for selfish reasons, I say it's the greatest team," Jeter said. "I would put it up there against any team in history. And I would like our chances."

As usual, Jeter is right. The 1998 Yankees were a very talented, very focused, and very successful team, a club that exemplified what a team should be. They didn't have superstars or even All-Stars at every position, but they had an amazing nucleus, a talented supporting cast, and a steely-eyed focus. Watching the Yankees perform was like watching a group of pinstriped gentlemen who bullied the opposition, but who also dominated with dignity.

Of course, Jeter was the burgeoning star, the cool and handsome shortstop who actually dated pop star Mariah Carey that year and who did everything adeptly on the field. The kid wearing number 2 was beloved, especially by the kids who squealed over every move he made. Second baseman Chuck Knoblauch was a pest of a leadoff hitter whose postseason brain cramp created the most stressful moments of the year. But he and the Yankees survived and thrived.

On a passionate and focused team, the most intense player was right fielder Paul O'Neill, who treated every at-bat like it was his last and who treated watercoolers like they were punching bags. Much more relaxed than O'Neill was Bernie Williams, a switch-hitting center fielder who was committed to ending 1998 much differently than he ended 1997. Like O'Neill, Tino Martinez was another intense left-handed hitter who vanquished some postseason struggles with a memorable grand slam in the World Series. The catching position was shared by the fiery Jorge Posada and the intelligent Joe Girardi, two dedicated men behind the plate.

From the unlikely hero department, minor league lifer Shane Spencer swooped into the Bronx, invaded a potent lineup, and delivered a bunch of prodigious September swings. Scott Brosius was the biggest surprise of the season, a third baseman who rocketed from a .203 hitter in Oakland to a World Series MVP in New York. At various times, the bench included future Hall of Famer Tim Raines, Darryl Strawberry, and Chili Davis. In their careers, the trio combined for 6,386 hits, 855 homers, and 1,171 stolen bases. That's an iconic bench.

On the pitching staff, David Wells found a way to be perfect for one day and perfectly agitating to Manager Joe Torre on some other days. David Cone, the ultimate New York baseball player, treated Wells like a brother while also forming a dynamic one-two combo with him. Andy Pettitte was a ferocious competitor who won the clinching game of the World Series, even in a season where he grappled with some health issues in his family. Orlando "El Duque" Hernández, the gift of a pitcher from Cuba, brought grit and style to a juggernaut and also had youngsters in the New York area lifting their knees to their chins as they pitched.

With Rivera in the bullpen, Jeter often said, "When we go to Mo, we know the game is over." In that season, and in so many other seasons, it was. The Yankees lost only one game when they held a lead after eight innings. The stoic Rivera emphatically erased the disappointment of allowing a crushing homer in the 1997 postseason.

And guiding all the players was Torre, the man who Jeter called "the perfect manager" for this team. After a sluggish start in the first week led to some dubious questions about Torre's job security, he chastised the Yankees during a memorable team meeting in Seattle. The Yankees responded like a bulldozer rolling over an aluminum can, causing Torre to say he had never managed a team that simply refused to lose even one game.

Twenty-five years after that historic season, I revisited it with the players who churned through a season like none they had ever experienced. These interviews provide new perspectives and new insights about that spectacular season, from how they bonded (quickly) to how they squabbled (not too often) to how they soared (often). Over and over, the players marveled at what they had accomplished. Time, it was clear, had made them even prouder.

"It's the greatest team ever," said Wells. "There's no doubt. Just look at the depth we had."

O'Neill added, "It was as close to a perfect team as I've ever been around."

Finally, Torre said, "I think I managed the best team of all-time."

I coauthored a book called *The Life You Imagine* with Jeter while he was still playing and there were topics he simply didn't want to discuss. In contrast, he was thrilled to discuss the historical placing of the 1998 Yankees. After noting how the Yankees didn't have a player who hit even 30 homers that year, Jeter returned to the theme of how deep, versatile, and deadly they were. He stressed how the Yankees could "beat you in so many different ways" and how they could still excel when a few players were struggling.

"So when I say I would put us up there against any team, what I mean is that every team goes through times where they scuffle," Jeter added. "But, if we had two or three guys who were struggling, somebody else would always step up."

And then Jeter said something I'll never forget.

"We," Jeter said, "wanted to pummel teams."

Pummel teams. Not just beat them, but pummel them. And they did. As Jeter explained, somebody would always produce for the Yankees. All the way to a 125–50 record, which is engraved on the left shank of their World Series championship rings. And all the way to asserting themselves as the greatest team of all time. Jeter knows.

"I still don't think anyone's going to do what we did," Jeter said. "Not 125–50. I don't think it will be done again."

CHAPTER 1

Before Glory, Suffering

The baseball gods were taunting the Yankees, stalking them and scaring them. On a crisp October night in Cleveland, they mocked the defending champions, telling them their season was almost over. The Yankees had one lonely out left.

One more chance. Just one more chance to save themselves. That's what the Yankees were hoping to do against the Indians. And, after Paul O'Neill's scorching line drive off the right field fence and his sprawling dive into second base for a double, the Yankees had that chance. They were still hopeful of winning the 1997 Division Series and Bernie Williams was the player who carried that snippet of a hope to the plate.

Always thoughtful, always patient, and much more tenacious than he looked, Williams had seemed unsettled while managing two hits in 16 at-bats in the series. But Williams, who was armed with a 32-ounce bat, had the chance to redeem himself with one smooth swing against Jose Mesa. Williams took deep breaths and told himself to get a pitch that he could handle. A single would tie the game. For the Yankee faithful, Bernie, the reliable and likable Bernie, held all their hopes.

Baseball is a fulfilling and a deflating sport, a game that can be replete with endless joy or perpetual dread. And all of that can happen in one at-bat. In the moment that Williams faced Mesa, everyone in both dugouts, everyone in the press box, and all 45,203 fans knew that this at-bat would either end the game or extend the game. It would help decide which team advanced to the American League Championship Series and which team packed to go home—a baseball family abruptly departing in 25 divergent paths.

Tall and thick and sporting a handlebar mustache, Mesa was a reliever who threw hard and had a nasty slider. On the first pitch of the at-bat, the right-hander fired a slider that hung in the strike zone. It was the kind of pitch that Williams could have hammered. Williams, a switch-hitter who was batting from the left side, swung and lifted the ball toward left center field, his eyes, the catcher's eyes, and the umpire's eyes simultaneously peering in that direction. Could it find a gap? Would it land untouched? Were the Yankees still breathing?

Williams loped out of the batter's box, laying his bat on the grass as he moved. After about six steps, he looked down and toward the first base dugout, the body language of a concerned hitter. He kept running to first and looking left. Running and looking. And, of course, hoping. By the time Williams had taken a dozen steps, the inevitable agony arrived as the ball was caught by left fielder Brian Giles. Williams, his hope now gone, shook his head and shouted, "Nooooooo!"

Before Glory, Suffering

On the television broadcast, play-by-play man Joe Buck said simply, "Into left center. Giles is there. Celebrate."

Cleveland, not New York, celebrated. At 11:47 p.m. on October 6, 1997, the proud and mighty Yankees, who had won it all during an inspiring 1996, lost the fifth game of the series, 4–3, and were eliminated from the postseason. They were no longer defending their championship. It was painful and perplexing, especially since the Yankees were only four outs away from winning Game 4 and the series with Mariano Rivera on the mound.

But, as wrenching as that series loss was, I've always believed that the Yankees' march toward a historic 1998 began shortly after midnight.

Those devastating feelings immediately motivated them to not be in that position again.

The motivation to succeed comes in a variety of forms and from a variety of places. With the Yankees of that era, several players said that their motivation stemmed from themselves, from their teammates, from principal owner George Steinbrenner, from the news media, and from any other source or slight that can compel an athlete to perform better. For the 1998 Yankees who were part of that 1997 team, that loss, that crushing defeat to Cleveland, was as motivating as anything else.

Before the Yankees could win an unprecedented 125 games, before they could outscore opponents by 309 runs, before they could feature nine regulars who all had a .350 on-base percentage or higher, and before they could thrust themselves into the conversation about being the greatest team of all time, there had to be a loss in 1997.

Before there was history, there had to be some misery.

"That loss in '97 drove us," said catcher Jorge Posada. "It was just a mindset of never letting that happen again."

Reliever Jeff Nelson couldn't escape the notion of what the Yankees had left behind in Cleveland. Everything.

"I think 1997 was a humbling experience for all of us," Nelson said. "You go to the World Series and win in 1996 and you're on the top of the world. The one thing that happens is you can never be complacent in New York. I think you might be able to do that in other places, but not in New York. In New York, you can't just be satisfied with winning it one time. And I think that's great. I think that's the way it should be. I think that's something we learned in 1997. We thought we were going to walk right in and say, 'Hey, we're going to beat Cleveland and here we go again.' And it didn't work out that way. So it hurts you and it humbles you."

After Williams's fly ball landed in Giles's glove, the Yankees were a bewildered, morose bunch. Derek Jeter, who grounded out against Mesa in the ninth, sat stone-faced in the dugout clutching a towel, his batting gloves still on. Perhaps he was envisioning another at-bat, another chance. "I wasn't ready to stop playing," he said.

Tino Martinez, who had slugged a team-high 44 homers that season, which was the most by a Yankees' first baseman since Lou Gehrig in 1936, sat beside Jeter, his glove tucked under his right arm. "A horrible loss," Martinez said.

On the field in front of them, the Indians celebrated. Rivera was in a lonely place, a first-year closer who failed to close and who lamented how he had allowed a game-tying homer to Sandy Alomar Jr. in the eighth inning of Game 4. The Yankees needed four more outs from Rivera, but they lost that game and then lost the deciding game by a run when Williams made the final out.

"Paul O'Neill almost broke his neck sliding into second base with one of those disastrous slides," Williams said. "And then it was up to me to keep the game going. And I failed miserably."

Failed miserably. That's not an easy thing for anyone to say, especially for a sublime and elite athlete like Williams. But Williams took that negative, that ubiquitous negative, and brought it with him into the off-season. And every time he lifted weights, ran sprints, swung a bat, threw a baseball, or even gulped a bottle of water, he thought about Mesa and that "lazy fly ball" that pierced Williams's heart and psyche.

"I took that so hard that I trained like I'd never trained before in the off-season, mentally and physically," Williams said. "I told myself I was going to be better prepared if that situation ever happened again. Physically, I got myself ready. But mentally, I put myself in a mindset where I was going to be the best clutch hitter I could be. And that attitude catapulted me into having the year I had in 1998."

Mesa, who had conquered Williams, had a lot to ponder in the off-season too. Twenty days after subduing Williams, Mesa had the chance to guide the Indians to their first World Series title since 1948, which meant he had a chance to forever be a hero in a city aching for baseball glory. But Mesa allowed a run and blew a save against the Florida Marlins in the ninth inning and the Indians eventually lost in 11 innings in Game 7. Mesa's dread was even more depressing than Williams's dread. Baseball. Exhilarating one day. Deflating three weeks later. Williams knew Mesa's pain because it was the same kind of pain.

"Baseball kind of fancies itself by this notion that we play so many games that you always have an opportunity to vindicate yourself," Williams said. "If something bad happened to you the day before, you always have the chance to say, 'Hey, I'll get them tomorrow.' After I made that last out, there was no tomorrow until the next year. It was one of the hardest things I've ever had to face in the game."

As the Yankees trudged off the field and returned to the clubhouse, they were speechless. It was a startlingly quiet scene, one that was accentuated by Manager Joe Torre. Torre needed to be with his players. So he exited the manager's office and turned left to get to the clubhouse, noticing how somber it felt. No one was speaking. So Torre didn't speak either. Instead, Torre found a chair, sat down in the middle of the room, and joined his players in essentially bidding adieu to the 1997 season. For several minutes, Torre shared the silence with his players.

"There was nothing I could say to them about the season," Torre said. "There was no one to blame. I just had to peel Bernie Williams off the dugout steps because he was do distraught. It was a stunner. We all felt that we let something get away from us."

The minutes drifted off the clock. Five minutes. Ten minutes. Fifteen minutes. Different players have different recollections of how long Torre sat with them in the noiseless clubhouse, but David Cone said it felt like it lasted as long as an hour. It wasn't an hour because reporters were soon allowed in the room to interview the Yankees, but it felt endless because it was such a powerful display. Without saying a word, Torre and the Yankees were holding a vigil for their now completed season, a season that they thought would end with another title.

"It was like a funeral," Cone said. "Torre just sat there after that loss. You expected him to say something like, 'We fought hard. I'm proud of you.' But he didn't say a word. You could see his eyes moving around the room and he was looking at everybody. Eventually, he just got up and walked up to every single player and thanked them and gave them a hug. Every single player. I thought it was tremendous. There was nothing to say. His nonverbal eye contact and the way he hugged everybody was better than any-thing he could have said. It was respect. Pure respect."

After Torre was finished saying thanks and offering hugs, there were interviews to be done, reflections to be offered, and emotions to be unloaded. O'Neill, who had a spectacular series with a .421 average (8 for 19) and two homers, sat by his locker, a maze of microphones in his face, and said what everyone was feeling. Sure, every player could think about what he might have done differently to change an outcome, O'Neill said. But then he aptly and bluntly concluded, "It's all over now." And it was all over, except for the lingering pain. O'Neill theorized that it would take "about four months" to get over the loss. O'Neill set-tled on four months of grieving because that would take him to February 1998, the next time the Yankees would all gather in a clubhouse together. Basically, O'Neill planned to sulk and stew from Halloween to Thanksgiving to Christmas to New Year's Day to Valentine's Day and, well, you get the idea. This loss was everlasting. This loss was ever-present. And motivating.

Back in the clubhouse, other than spikes being tossed onto the floor or players speaking in hushed tones, the room remained mostly silent. Steinbrenner was a fixture in the clubhouse during this series because he always wanted to be around the team for the most important games, the old college football coach in him emerging as he offered up his version of support and motivation. Before the game, Steinbrenner, who was born in Ohio, rode an elevator with some reporters and said he had a positive feeling about Game 5.

"This is what sports is all about," he said, before his Yankees landed on the wrong side of that outcome.

Never hesitant to give his unfiltered assessments of his players, his coaches, or his manager, Steinbrenner played a different role on this depressing night. He was a consoler. The owner circled the clubhouse and patted the players on their backs and told them how proud he was of what they had accomplished. Steinbrenner told O'Neill how valuable he had been and how fortunate the Yankees were to have him. By the way, the Boss started calling him "the Warrior" after that daring dash to second. But O'Neill didn't want to hear those compliments. His bat and his glove were going into storage.

Once Steinbrenner finished comforting his players, all 25 of them, he turned from a consoler to a predictor.

"We'll win it next year," Steinbrenner said. "Mark my words."

I was standing near Steinbrenner as he uttered those memorable words and, as I scribbled them into a notebook, I thought it was the kind of statement an owner would and should make. It was a way to give these forlorn Yankees some hope, even if none of the players heard him. It was also a message to Yankee fans. But, in that moment, those words, which would eventually and emphatically prove to be true, didn't resonate. The Yankees were still mourning. The future was unwritten. And next season, the season that ended up being glorious and gratifying, seemed so far away.

Before Glory, Suffering

On the Yankees' flight from Cleveland to New York, Martinez remembered one overwhelming factor: more silence. Normally, even after a frustrating loss, players eventually begin to talk during the journey. There are some card games, some banter about what just happened, and maybe some thoughts about vacation plans. But there was little of that on this flight. For the entire trip home, the Yankees were on mute.

"That series was a horrible loss for us because we won in 1996 and we thought that we were a better team in 1997," Martinez said. "In fact, we knew that we were better in 1997 than in 1996. So we totally expected to win the World Series again. That was our goal and our only goal. Anything less than that was disappointing. To lose that series the way we did, with Alomar hitting a homer off Mo. Yeah, we let one go there in 1997."

Understanding how despondent the Yankees were, Cone decided to try and help the players share in their torment for a few more hours. He contacted a friend who owned a bar in the West Village section of Manhattan and asked if the man could keep the doors open and keep the taps flowing for the wounded Yankees. And Cone's friend agreed to accommodate the Yankees. It was a caring act by Cone, the kind of act that was all about leadership. Cone knew he would be awake for hours as he ruminated about how the Yankees lost in Cleveland. So he might as well share the what-ifs with his teammates.

The bar gathering backfired on Cone as much as if he had placed his pitching hand over a flame. The person whom Cone had considered a friend allowed pictures to be taken of the distraught Yankees at that bar and they didn't look too distraught. They looked like party animals. That became apparent to many because the *New York Post* ended up with the partying pictures and published them and an article with the headline "YANKEE PANKY." The subhead read, "BOMBERS PARTY THE NIGHT AWAY AFTER LOSING TO THE TRIBE." Gulp.

Once the pictures were in the *Post*, Cone received a phone call from an angry Steinbrenner. The Boss told Cone that he and his Yankee teammates didn't behave like true Yankees and that the pictures made it seem as if they didn't care about the awful way the season had ended. Cone explained to Steinbrenner that he realized how bad it looked and that it was his decision, no one else's, to go to the bar and bond over the season one last time. Steinbrenner listened to Cone and accepted the explanation, but he ended the call by telling Cone he was disappointed.

Back at Yankee Stadium, less than 24 hours after the Yankees' season ended, the mourning continued. The day after a postseason loss is always "clean-out" day or "pack-up" day. Players will trickle into the clubhouse, stuff their belongings into cardboard boxes, and say goodbye until spring training.

"I thought we were going to win the whole thing," said pitcher David Wells. "My stomach was hurting because I thought we were going all the way. I really thought this was going to be a storybook finish."

Sitting behind his desk in the manager's office, the eloquent Torre quoted his mother in saying that "everything happens for a reason" and, sometimes, that reason isn't immediately apparent. But, Torre concluded, "If you beat yourself up and think why did this happen or why did that happen, you'll go nuts."

In the aftermath of the loss, Torre, who was still managing his players and their emotions, had a tender conversation with Rivera on the tarmac at Newark Airport. At that point, Rivera was a new closer with a glistening future, but he was not yet the pitcher who would notch the final out for five World Series titles or who would become the first and only player to be voted into the Hall of Fame unanimously. He was still a 27-year-old trying to figure out how an outside fastball turned into his worst nightmare and who was calling the loss his fault. Torre told Rivera that he was one of the primary reasons the Yankees were even in position to succeed in the postseason, so he should not think he was the reason the Yankees faltered.

"I just wanted him to know what we felt about him and how there was so much more for him to celebrate than there was for him to be depressed about," Torre said. "What happened to him was just one of those things. It's tough to create what Mariano became without first having a belly full of guts."

Rivera appreciated Torre's wisdom and realized he needed to look ahead.

"I was kind of feeling guilty the other day when we lost," Rivera said. "I still feel a little guilty, but I have to let it go. You can't look back. It won't be easy."

As boxes were packed and taped on that good-bye day at the stadium, the person I remember more than any players was a custodian who was carrying a gallon of white paint, a brush, and a ladder. He shuffled through the bowels of the stadium and eventually stopped at a staircase that was adjacent to the players' entrance. I didn't know the man's name, but I was dumbfounded as I watched him climb the ladder, dip the brush in the paint, and carefully paint over the blue "1996 World Champions" on the cinderblock wall.

"It's a shame," the man said. "I hate having to do this. That darn game killed me."

The Yankees were STILL the 1996 champions. There shouldn't have been any rush or, honestly, any desire to paint over those words. Heck, the Yankees could have left those words up for infinity because they would always be the 1996 champs. But in Steinbrenner's world, 1997 had been a failure. So the championship reminder, a proud remembrance of a glorious season, was removed with several strokes of a paintbrush. For the custodian, that was as crushing as the loss itself.

On that bleak day, Torre revealed that he slept only four hours because, oddly enough, his bedroom was being painted and he needed to wake up early and vacate his house. When Torre was told that Steinbrenner predicted a championship for 1998, the manager said, "I expect to win too. It makes it tougher when you expect to win when you don't know who your players are. When the Boss says that, it means he's going to get you the players."

Expecting to win? Getting the right players? Torre's words were just a forecast at that time, optimistic responses during a numbing period. While Torre and Steinbrenner didn't yet know it, the Yankees were going to have perhaps the greatest collection of players the organization had ever assembled. None of us knew it, but 1998 was going to be an illuminating and remarkable season in Yankeeland. The Yankees would play in a way that no team had ever played. They would play like the best team of all time. Even the baseball gods would be in awe.

CHAPTER 2

The Pieces of the Puzzle

The blue carpet had been freshly vacuumed, the folding chairs were all neatly assembled by the players' lockers, and the uniforms were all pressed and hanging on hooks in the lockers. It was a pristine scene in the Yankees' clubhouse in February 1998, the start of another spring training day in Tampa. Like every spring, it was a time of hope and optimism for the Yankees. The goal, as always, was to be the last team standing and smiling after winning a title in October.

Everyone who was in the clubhouse knew that, from the players to the coaches to the attendants who had just hung up those uniforms. That was the Yankee mandate because that was principal owner George Steinbrenner's dictate. Unless the Yankees won a World Series championship, Steinbrenner considered the season a failure. That might seem too demanding, but that's the way Steinbrenner felt and that's the way he wanted everyone in the organization to feel. And, remember, Steinbrenner had vowed four months earlier that the Yankees would win it all in 1998.

When Joe Torre emerged from his office on this day and sauntered a few steps into the clubhouse, he was starting his third full season as manager of the Yankees. It was a position he adored and a position that had helped rejuvenate his career. After Torre guided the Yankees to the World Series in 1996, it was the first time in his 32-year career that he had been involved in the Fall Classic, as a player or as a manager. When the Yankees won, Torre wept. A lot.

There were no tears from Torre on this morning. But there was a message from the manager. It was a simple yet serious message that everyone in the room already knew and probably expected. But it still mattered.

"We," Torre said, "have unfinished business."

In Torre's first full-squad meeting of the year, he reminded the players about 1997 and reminded them about what they had NOT accomplished. He talked about failure before he talked about expectations. He wanted them to think about the agony of 1997 before he mentioned the hopefulness of 1998. It was intentional, it was smart, and it was well-received.

"You're talking about a lot of guys on that team who knew what happened and knew what we had to do," said catcher Jorge Posada. "But as soon as Joe said that we had unfinished business, it just immediately put you in a certain mindset. It was like, 'OK. Here we go.'"

Sitting in a chair near the back wall of the clubhouse, Posada peered to his left and to his right after he heard Torre's words. He knew that those words resonated with Derek Jeter, Bernie Williams, Paul O'Neill, Mariano Rivera, David Cone, and the rest of the Yankees from the 1997 team. He was glad

Torre said it because it told the Yankees, new and old, there needed to be an urgency in the way they performed.

"It was great to hear that from Joe, but we knew what we had to do and we knew that we should have won in 1997," said first baseman Tino Martinez. "We had that good of a team."

I've covered spring training for more than 30 years and players are sometimes resistant to talk about the previous season, especially if it had a sour ending. While the Yankees could have distanced themselves from questions about the 1997 loss to the Indians, they didn't. Several players embraced the questions, understanding what it meant and how it could guide them.

"When you're faced with tough times, it helps to talk about it," Posada said. "Believe it or not, by talking about it and by getting it out in the open, that helps you forget about it. And it helps you move on from it."

For the new Yankees like Chuck Knoblauch, Scott Brosius, and Chili Davis, Torre's words about "unfinished business" didn't resonate as much because they played for other teams in 1997 and weren't part of that postseason loss. Or maybe Torre's words did resonate with them. Jeter said the first-year Yankees "could sense" just how focused, dedicated, and committed the Yankees were to creating a much better ending in 1998. And those new players also understood they were imported to be a part of that new and better script.

Twenty-three players appeared in at least one game for the 1997 team and the 1998 team and 15 men played for the 1996, 1997, and 1998 teams. That continuity is another reason why Jeter said the new additions were quickly and keenly aware of how their hungry and unfulfilled teammates felt about this season. Everywhere those players looked in the clubhouse, there was someone lamenting 1997 and swearing that it would never happen again.

"I think losing that series was a carryover for all of the guys who were there in '97," Jeter said. "And it was especially true for the guys who were there in '96 and '97 because we're coming from winning the World Series and it's the ultimate elation, and then we're going through 1997 where it's the ultimate disappointment. And no one wanted to experience that again. And I think the new players that came in, I think they felt it."

Roaming from field to field and from meeting to meeting that spring was the Yankees' new general manager: Brian Cashman. Even though Cashman had been the assistant GM for the previous five seasons and first worked for the Yankees in 1986, he never expected to be in this position. There is a Talking Heads song called "Once in a Lifetime" that includes the lyrics, "And you may ask yourself, 'Well, how did I get here?'"

That question applied to Cashman. Well, how did he get here?

On a sleepy Monday morning in early February, Cashman was on a conference call with the American League's scheduling committee from his Yankee Stadium office. Once, twice, and then three times, General Manager Bob Watson poked his head into Cashman's office because he wanted to chat. Cashman wondered what was so urgent. As soon as Cashman completed the two-hour call, Watson returned. He closed the door to Cashman's office.

"And that's when he told me he had resigned the night before," Cashman said. "He said that it was for health reasons and that he talked it over with his wife and how the best thing for him was to shut it down."

Cashman paused, slowly piecing together the words that came next.

"After Bob told the Boss he had resigned, he told me he had recommended I replace him," Cashman said. "And I specifically remember him saying to me, 'You're going to have a lot to think about, buddy.'"

Cashman was stunned. At that time, the GM job was still mostly filled by former players. But, even more critically, Cashman had witnessed how the demanding and blustery Steinbrenner had treated Watson and Gene "Stick" Michael when they were GMs, so he recognized how challenging the job was. As Cashman tried to absorb everything that was swirling around him, he also tried to change Watson's mind.

"So I spent 15 minutes trying to convince him to un-resign," Cashman said. "I begged Bob Watson not to leave. And that's when he kept repeating, 'You're going to have a lot to think about, buddy. I think he's going to call you today.'"

Soon after that conversation, Steinbrenner called and asked Cashman if he had spoken with Watson. Cashman said they had spoken.

"OK, that's good," Steinbrenner responded. "Can you meet with me? I'm at the Regency. How's 2 p.m.?"

Cashman told Steinbrenner he would be at the Regency Hotel, which is on Park Avenue in Manhattan, by two. But, as the words came out of Cashman's mouth, he was still in shock. Instantly, Cashman said he realized "my whole world was about to turn upside down."

The meeting with Steinbrenner, a meeting that really would change Cashman's sleeping patterns and, well, his life forever, was quick and businesslike.

"You know what's going on," Steinbrenner said. "Bob has resigned and he has strongly recommended that you replace him. I could go out and recycle someone who has already had this job, but I've spoken to enough people who have told me you're ready for this. So I'm offering you the opportunity to be the general manager of the New York Yankees."

What was Cashman's first thought?

"I was scared shitless," he said.

Scared beyond belief? Yes. Scared enough or foolish enough to say no to the tempting offer? Absolutely not.

"I had too much respect for that chair to think I could automatically do the job," Cashman said. "I had never aspired to do it. If anything, I had been on the front lines enough to realize that was not a job I would want to do. But, at the same time, I was smart enough to realize this was an opportunity I couldn't turn down. So I said yes."

Moving forward with the discussion, Steinbrenner tried to talk about the terms of Cashman's contract. It was the one time Cashman took control of the negotiations.

"How about we just do a one-year, non-guaranteed contract?" Cashman said.

Steinbrenner liked that idea and agreed. Cashman was betting on himself while also giving himself a lifeboat if he really despised being a GM. At 30 years old, he became the second-youngest GM in baseball history after San Diego's Randy Smith, who became the Padres' GM at 29. Steinbrenner boosted Cashman's salary from $85,000 to $130,000.

"The Boss put a salary number out there and then we shook hands and that was it," Cashman said. "It was the quickest negotiation I've ever had."

Affable, prepared, and tough, Cashman began working for the Yankees as an intern in the security department in 1986. Since John Cashman, Brian's father, was a racetrack owner and horse breeder from Lexington, Kentucky, he knew Steinbrenner, another horse owner. Knowing how baseball-crazed Brian was, the elder Cashman asked Alan Finkelson, a mutual friend, to find out if Steinbrenner had an opening for Brian. And that's how the 160-pound Cashman landed in a security job. The future GM broke up a fight or two in the stands at Yankee Stadium before he ever signed a free agent or two.

As a second baseman at Catholic University in Washington, Cashman set the school record for most hits in a season with 52. (It has since been broken.) Cashman was hired by the Yankees as a baseball operations assistant in 1989, was promoted to farm director in 1990, and became a major league administrator in 1993. He was an assistant under Michael and Watson after that. At his introductory press conference, Cashman conceded that evaluating player talent wasn't his strength. He was a solid negotiator and administrator. And, in February 1998, he was suddenly in charge of the Yankees and was suddenly the man who would receive the angry calls from Steinbrenner, calls where the Boss wanted immediate answers.

"Hands-on owners get involved," Cashman said. "I knew that. I'd lived that."

Indeed. Cashman watched Watson grow weary of the endless hours and the endless harangues from Steinbrenner. Quite often, Steinbrenner overruled Watson (and other GMs) and acted as his own GM in pushing to make baseball decisions. In April 1997, Watson was hospitalized for high blood pressure and ordered to reduce his workload by 25 percent. That meant he worked 80-hour weeks instead of 105-hour weeks. At one point, Watson said, "I'm not willing to kill myself for this job."

Michael, who was the first GM Cashman assisted and who was one of the executives Steinbrenner trusted the most, once playfully told Cashman that George took the credit for all of the wins and Michael received the blame for all of the losses.

"It kind of feels that way when you're the Yankee GM," Cashman said.

Because Cashman had grown up in the Yankees organization, the Yankee way and the Steinbrenner way was all he had ever known. Cashman had watched how his predecessors had dealt with Steinbrenner and the excessive responsibilities of the position, so he knew those same demands would be placed on him. As much as Cashman said he never wanted the GM position, an energetic 30-year-old who had several years of experience with Steinbrenner's style was, in many ways, the perfect person for the job.

Three days after Cashman replaced Watson, the Yankees acquired Knoblauch from the Minnesota Twins for left-handed pitcher Eric Milton, shortstop Cristian Guzmán, two other minor leaguers, and $3 million. It was a necessary move and a move that had been speculated about ever since the Yankees' season ended in Cleveland. Knoblauch had grown disenchanted with losing in Minnesota and told the Twins that he wanted to be traded to a contender.

One day after the Yankees lost to the Indians, I wrote this in the *New York Times*: "But the Yankees should field a very talented team that contends again and might even improve if George Steinbrenner spruces up the roster by adding Robin Ventura at third or Chuck Knoblauch at second." Two months after that, I asked Cone, one of the most influential voices on the Yankees, about Knoblauch and the pitcher was smitten. "I think when you hear some of the comments Chuck has made and how he wants to come here and wants to be a Yankee, that rings loud and clear," Cone said. "He's a special player. If you have a chance to get him, I think you have to do it." A few days later, I reached Knoblauch at his home in Houston and he was just as keen with the idea of playing for the Yankees.

"I think New York would be a great place to play," Knoblauch said. "When you open the season, you want to know you're going to be competitive and going to have the chance to win. I think if you ask any Yankee players right now, they'll tell you they got a chance to win. I think every player wants that."

And Knoblauch also displayed some verbal swagger.

"I think it would be pretty intriguing," he said. "Nothing against Luis Sojo or anyone else they have, but I can play second. If it were to happen, I wouldn't gripe."

It happened. In Knoblauch, the Yankees felt they had obtained one of the best second basemen in the major leagues, a player who would become entrenched at the top of the order and whose career was on a Hall of Fame trajectory. Knoblauch won a World Series title with the Twins in 1991 and also won the Rookie of the Year Award that season. In addition, Knoblauch had made three All-Star teams and had also won a Gold Glove Award. He was exactly what the Yankees needed: a feisty leadoff hitter who took a lot of pitches, who could work walks and smack hits, who could steal bases, and who played intensely. Knoblauch exhausted pitches. He saw 4.09 pitches per plate appearance in 1998, second best on the team to Darryl Strawberry's 4.23.

"It was a new beginning for me," Knoblauch said. "I knew I was going to a good team. They won the World Series in '96. And I don't know what happened to them in '97, really. But I was happy to be there."

Backup infielder Homer Bush understood his chances of making the 25-man roster had decreased after the Knoblauch trade because it was one more player with a guaranteed contract. But, as a realist, he understood the impact of the move.

"When he got traded to us, he was still the man," Bush said. "This was before his career started to go into a decline. When he came to us, I would have bet the house he was going to the Hall of Fame. I would have swapped my firstborn to make that bet because this dude would just hit and play defense. He was a human highlight reel."

During Knoblauch's first week with the Yankees, he learned that the passion of some players wasn't limited to the field. After a workout, Knoblauch returned to a mostly empty clubhouse and heard the soft strumming of a guitar.

As Knoblauch sidled up to his locker, which was near Jeter's locker, he spotted Williams playing his guitar. Knoblauch wasn't accustomed to being teammates with a center fielder who doubled as a musician and, at first, he didn't say anything. He just listened. Eventually, Williams spoke.

"Let me open a window to your mind," Williams said to Knoblauch, "and let you in."

The philosophical nature of Williams's invitation startled Knoblauch, who stayed silent and kept listening. That's what Williams wanted all along.

"He didn't say anything else to me," Knoblauch said. "I think he was just going to let the music speak for him. And, as I got to know him, I found out that it turned out to be the perfect line from Bernie."

Besides the addition of Knoblauch, the Yankees also made a trade for another infielder. When the Yankees announced the transaction on November 7, 1997, it was described this way: Traded left-handed pitcher Kenny Rogers and cash considerations to Oakland for a player to be named later.

Yes, in the initial disclosure of the deal for Scott Brosius, his name was excluded.

Somehow, that seems appropriate because the acquisition of Brosius was an under-the-radar move for the Yankees that turned out to be magnificent. As part of the agreement, the A's agreed to protect Brosius in the upcoming expansion draft, which is why he wasn't identified in the announcement.

Since Brosius hit .203 with the 1997 A's, the move was considered more of a salary dump and a way to jettison Rogers, who in two years had shown that he was not equipped to handle New York or all that came with being on Steinbren-ner's team. The Yankees included $5 million in the deal. With the A's, Brosius had stretches in which he went 0 for 17 and 0 for 20 and 3 for 41. He hit .181 in April and then got even worse when he hit .147 in May. It took him 87 at-bats before he hit his first homer in 1997.

Still, Ron Brand, a West Coast scout for the Yankees, was steadfast in his support of Brosius and told Cashman, "I believe in this kid and I think he will bounce back." At best, Brand told Cashman that Brosius would be the starting third baseman. At worst, Brand told Cashman that Brosius, who had played five positions for the A's, would be a dependable utility player who could adequately replace Randy Velarde.

"Ron Brand was right," Cashman said. "Everything he said was right."

And Brosius?

"Brosius was spectacular," Cashman said. "He was a gift from above."

The backup infielder for the Yankees was Sojo, who was as nice and as popular as anyone in the clubhouse. Chronically smiling and teasing his teammates, Sojo was a slick fielder who was also an astute baseball man. In 1997, Sojo asked Posada if he thought Jeter would be receptive to some advice about the way Jeter turned double plays. Posada quickly said that Jeter would listen to Sojo, who had tutored Álex Rodrí-guez in Seattle.

That exchange led to Sojo telling Jeter he was putting in too much effort and was potentially putting himself in danger by leaping over the sliding base runner as he cut across second base to turn double plays. Sojo told Jeter he should position himself behind the base to protect himself because no base runners slide hard across the base. They slide hard into the base. As the throw came to Jeter at second, Sojo taught him to touch the base with his right foot and then pivot toward the outfield. It made the play so much easier for Jeter. Once Sojo suggested that adjustment, Jeter welcomed the guidance and asked Sojo to work with him on a daily basis.

"I was the type of guy who never liked to get to the ballpark that early, like at 1:30," Sojo said. "I always liked to get there at 3:30, right before we stretched. So Posada talked to Jeter and that was a big mistake on my part because I had to be at the ballpark at 1:30 every single day for like a month."

After recounting that story, Sojo laughed. He was always laughing. Of course, he was joking. He loved teaching the intricacies of playing the infield and loved watching how Jeter implemented the changes. But Sojo didn't love being called into the manager's office, which is what happened to him in spring training in 1998.

Torre knew the importance of allowing Brosius to get acclimated to New York and getting off to a fast start, which is why the manager needed to speak with Sojo. As much as Sojo expected his at-bats to be scarce, he was surprised by Torre's message.

"You need to keep yourself prepared," Torre said, "because you're not going to play in April."

"What?" a confused Sojo asked.

Torre explained, "Knoblauch is going to play 140 games. Tino is going to play 140 games. Jeter is going to play 150 games. And I have to see what Brosius can do so he needs to play every day. Just keep yourself ready."

Sojo exited the office and jokingly said, "I almost killed myself. But you've got to realize that you've got to be ready to do your job. You've got to understand your role. And that's what I did with the Yankees."

A few days before Opening Day, Sojo fractured his left hand and went on the disabled list on March 30, which opened a roster spot for Bush. Instead of Sojo watching from the dugout as Brosius became acclimated, it was Bush who served as the backup infielder and full-time spectator. He didn't start his first game until May 3. By the end of May, Brosius was hitting .333 with a .401 on base percentage and a .462 slugging percentage. Torre's decision to play Brosius a lot had worked wondrously. Brosius started 147 games at third base in 1998, the most by a Yankees' third baseman since Graig Nettles started 159 in 1978.

How reliable and productive was Brosius? The Yankees signed Dale Sveum to a two-year, $1.6 million deal as an insurance policy in case Brosius sputtered. And Sveum wound up being a very observant and nonplaying Yankee. As Sveum noted, "I never ended up playing because he played so well and everyone else stayed healthy."

A month after the Brosius deal, the Yankees signed designated hitter Chili Davis to a three-year, $9.8 million contract. Davis was the only DH Steinbrenner wanted and he fit the hitting profile the Yankees liked with his blend of power and patience. With the Kansas City Royals in 1997, Davis hit .278 with 30 homers and 90 runs batted in, but he also walked 85 times while striking out 99 times.

"We're very happy with this guy because he's a tremendous hitter and a tremendous influence in the clubhouse," Steinbrenner explained. "We thought one of our problems last year was moving from DH to DH. You look at Davis and he's a professional DH. That's what we lacked last year."

As confident as the Yankees were in Jeter, Williams, O'Neill, and Martinez, they knew they needed to improve their roster for 1998. And they did that in ways both big and small. The additions of Knoblauch, Brosius, and Davis were savvy moves, even if the wise Davis played only 35 games. Knoblauch and Brosius were linchpin players, starters who produced every day and who fit the Yankees' workmanlike approach.

"It's very unusual to have a team that's egoless," Knoblauch said. "I'd never been on a team like that in my career. It was a great feeling to know that everybody was there to win it. And that was it. Win at any cost."

With a returning core of talented players, some stellar additions, and a desire to avenge what happened in 1997, the Yankees opened the season in Anaheim and lost to the Angels, 4–1. Steinbrenner had jokingly wondered if a team had ever gone 162–0. Was he really joking? And the Yankees lost their second game and third game too. It was the first time the Yankees had started 0–3 since 1985, which was the year in which Yogi Berra was fired after a lackluster 6–10 start.

Wait, could Torre, the soothing and popular manager, actually be in danger of losing his job? Some ink was spilled in the New York newspapers about this possibility, a seemingly ridiculous topic. There was no way Torre could actually be jettisoned. Was there? In typical Torre fashion, he dismissed the attention.

"If I start worrying about that, I'll manage scared and distracted, and I can't do that," Torre said.

Still, the players heard the same noise about Torre's status and it led to some restlessness in the clubhouse.

"I would call it an uneasy feeling," Cone said. "We all loved Joe and we all loved playing for Joe. We knew we should have been playing better and we knew it was unfair that anyone was talking about Joe's job."

Jeter added, "I didn't think Joe was really in trouble. You know how the New York media is. A lot of times, they blow things out of proportion a little bit. But you didn't want that narrative to continue because, if there's a narrative that continues for long stretches of time, you never know what's going to happen. But, after a handful of games, I didn't think he was in any danger of losing his job."

Finally and mercifully, the Yankees recorded their first win of the season by beating Oakland, 9–7. After Jeff Nelson snared the final out, he pumped his fist and celebrated with extra gusto. And why not? At that point, no team that had ever started the season with a 0–4 record had won the World Series. In 2021, the Atlanta Braves changed that.

"We were all shocked that we started 0–3," Nelson said. "We all knew we had a great team. We were wondering what the heck was going on. When we finally won, I was like, 'Hey, we won the World Series. Let's pop some champagne.'"

While Torre's job status continued to be discussed for several more days, what wasn't as commonly known is that Cashman probably came much closer to being fired by Steinbrenner. Cashman traveled to the West Coast with the Yankees in his first trip as the GM. It was supposed to be an exciting and memorable journey for Cashman, the first steps in his first season as the young phenom in the Yankees' front office.

Well, it was memorable, but not in the way Cashman had hoped. Once the Yanks lost their first three games by a combined score of 21–6, Steinbrenner needed someone to blame. Cashman became the target. The Boss was incensed and ordered Cashman to fly back to New York.

"Pack your bags and come home," Steinbrenner told Cashman.

Cashman didn't argue with Steinbrenner's directive. How could he fight the Boss? He had been on the job for only a couple of months. Cashman couldn't explain why a very good team had looked so beatable, albeit for a few games. So he listened to the Boss and flew home.

"He was furious," Cashman said. "And he ripped me out of the road trip."

Perturbed by the sluggish start, Steinbrenner pondered dismissing Cashman a few games into his tenure and replacing him with Michael, who had been the GM from 1980 to 1981 and from 1991 to 1995. Making an impulsive change was similar to what Steinbrenner almost did after hiring Torre as manager before the 1996 season. Soon after that hiring, Steinbrenner got antsy and met with Buck Showalter, whom Torre had replaced, and asked Showalter if he would be interested in returning. Steinbrenner had plans to slot Showalter in as the manager and would have made the freshly hired Torre an adviser. But Showalter declined Steinbrenner's overtures, so it never happened and, of course, the rest is history. Torre helped guide the Yankees to a championship in his first season as manager and won four titles in his first five seasons.

Mindful of how capricious Steinbrenner could be and knowing this wouldn't be the first time he would threaten to fire Cashman, Michael tried to reason with the Boss and to get him to relax. Obviously, Stick had experience with having been fired and rehired by the Boss. So, after emphatically saying no to returning as GM, he also reminded Steinbrenner how capable Cashman was and gave him a vote of confidence.

"I just remember I was supposed to be out there for the whole West Coast trip and I got pulled off of it and I was getting crushed," Cashman said. "Gene Michael told me the Boss asked him if he'd be willing to come back. And he said no. And Stick told me he told the Boss, 'This guy has got this. He'll be fine. Don't do that.' I didn't know any of that until later. Stick told me it later on, not right when it happened."

After the first win in Oakland, Torre and the Yankees' coaches signed the lineup card from the game and mailed it overnight to Cashman. If Cashman hadn't been sent home, Torre could have just handed him the card. At the top of the card, Torre referred to Cashman by his nickname and wrote "Crash: The first of many."

"That proved to be prophetic," Cashman said. "He said it was the first of many and that was win number one out of 125."

Cashman still has that lineup card. In fact, he donated it to the Yankees Museum and the card is on display at Yankee Stadium.

The celebratory feelings didn't linger as the Yankees lost to the Mariners to fall to 1–4. The Yankees struck out 15 times in a game started by the soft-tossing Jamie Moyer, and Torre, whether he was worried about his job or not, had seen enough. That night, Torre went to dinner by himself at the Metropolitan Grill in Seattle and decided the team had to play with more urgency. And Torre decided to deliver that message forcefully.

Before the sixth game of the season, Torre called a meeting in which he told the Yankees how upset he was with the way they were playing. Point by point and play by play, Torre, who rarely raised his voice in meetings, loudly told his players why they had disappointed him. Then Torre asked his players if any of them wanted to speak. And Cone, who was as respected as anyone in the clubhouse, sensed an opportunity to deliver a message to a team that was in a funk. It was a powerful team, maybe even a great team, and Cone wanted his teammates to feel like the badasses that he knew they were. So he stole something from another badass named Dave Parker.

Cone had heard Parker, a former MVP, say players need to find something they dislike about their opponents. So he found something for the Yankees to dislike about the Mariners. With his face turning red and his voice rising, Cone told the Yankees that Edgar Martinez had disrespected them by swinging from his heels at a 3–0 pitch and the Mariners leading, 4–0.

Was it a reach to call that disrespectful? Yes, it was.

But Cone needed to manufacture some anger.

"Number crunchers won't like hearing this, but I've seen those meetings work," Cone said. "I don't know how to quantify it, but I've experienced it. Those things can work. Not all the time, but they can't hurt."

Again, Cone was focused on despising the opponent.

"Especially when you're playing flat or struggling, you really need to hate your opponent," Cone added. "Is there an art or chemistry to getting out of those slumps? I don't know. Whether it's true or not that you really do hate your opponent, it doesn't matter. That approach can work. You just tell everybody, 'Hey, we're going to go out there and beat their ass today.'"

In the same game where Martinez swung at a 3–0 pitch, Moyer hit Paul O'Neill with a high-and-tight fastball that bounced off O'Neill's wrist. While Moyer who didn't have an overpowering fastball, the pitch was zooming toward O'Neill's head before it glanced off his hand. The close pitch infuriated the Yankees. Lou Piniella, the Mariners' manager, had been O'Neill's manager with the Cincinnati Reds and he reveled in having his pitchers throw inside to agitate O'Neill. Piniella had previously called O'Neill "a crybaby" for complaining when pitchers threw inside to him. Even though Moyer apologized about the pitch, the Yankees weren't happy with seeing Piniella's team dust O'Neill. Again. Cone didn't need to manufacture any anger about what Moyer did. The Yankees were pissed off.

"If we have to knock some guys down to get the message across, let's do it," Cone said in the meeting. "We need to have some dirt dog in us."

The Pieces of the Puzzle

Catcher Joe Girardi remembered the meeting being flooded with a lot of blunt talk "about protecting each other and being there for each other." Andy Pettitte, who pitched in the game where O'Neill was hit, apologized to O'Neill and wondered if he should have retaliated. While Girardi said the clubhouse was filled with love and respect, the players shared a lot of feelings about being more supportive of each other. And Girardi was also concerned about Torre's status if the Yankees continued to wobble.

"I think we felt bad about the way Joe was being treated because Joe was so important to us," Girardi said. "Joe was able to handle all of the distractions of New York and keep everything in the room. If we prepared, if we worked hard, and if we played hard, everything would take care of itself. That was Joe's message to us."

While Tino Martinez doesn't remember exactly what Torre said or every player who spoke that day, he does remember how Torre didn't fret. Even when Torre scolded or upbraided his players, he usually emitted a sense of confidence and a belief in them. Torre tried to be as emotionless as possible in the dugout because he never wanted his players to see him concerned about a situation. If Torre looked rattled, he thought that could adversely impact his players.

"What came out of that meeting for me was that Joe was not panicking," said Martinez. "When the season starts, you hope to get off to a good start because it takes time to get your timing down and for everybody to start clicking. And we weren't panicking and Joe wasn't panicking. And I don't think Joe was worried about his job. He just told us to keep playing hard and good things would happen."

And Torre also told the players that he would communicate with Steinbrenner and make sure the players didn't have to get involved in those discussions. Just play, Torre said.

"Joe always said, 'Don't worry, I'll take care of the Boss,'" Martinez said. "That's something he always told us. He'd say, 'You guys just go and play baseball and I will deal with the Boss.' Joe was great at keeping George in the loop on a daily basis. And that helped us as well. As long as our effort was there and we played to win, Joe never changed. It wasn't even about the wins and losses. It was about playing hard."

After Torre and his players had a rousing "Let's get it going" meeting, Knoblauch was the leadoff batter for the Yankees. He blasted Jim Bullinger's first pitch for a homer.

"I took the meeting to heart, I guess," Knoblauch said.

So did the rest of the Yankees. Jeter doubled. O'Neill had a run-scoring double. Bernie Williams whiffed, but Martinez socked an RBI single. Darryl Strawberry hammered a two-run homer. After a Tim Raines groundout, Jorge Posada belted a homer. Eight batters and 21 pitches into the game, the Yankees had a 6–0 lead over Bullinger, who would never pitch in the majors again after that night. The Yankees rampaged to a 13–7 victory, showing some anger and some swagger against the hated Mariners. The season wasn't even one week old, but that game was monumental.

"I think that was the shift right there," Knoblauch said. "I do remember that meeting. I don't remember everything that was said. But I know Joe told us, 'Guys, you've got to get it going.' And I remember that Coney talked a lot too."

The Yankees talked the talk that night and, soon, they

walked the walk. They beat the Mariners the next day, they returned to the Bronx and won their home opener, and they kept winning and winning. Steinbrenner cornered Torre at the Yankees' annual "Welcome Home" dinner and said, "You're my man," and rejected any thought of dismissing the manager. After Torre's meeting, the Yankees won 22 of their next 24 games and morphed into a juggernaut. As Cone said, sometimes getting angry at someone can boost a team. After the candid meeting in Seattle, the very deep and very talented Yankees also unleashed a scintillating streak in which they went 64–16 for an unfathomable winning percentage of .800.

"We joked about voting a full postseason share to Moyer because he was the pitcher who had knocked O'Neill down and that proved to be a wakeup call for us," Girardi said. "We took off after that."

Along this incredible journey that was developing for the Yankees, the one thing that did keep them from winning at Yankee Stadium was an unforeseen and unfortunate accident. On April 13, a 500-pound concrete and steel beam fell from the left field loge level and crashed into the empty seats. The falling expansion joint destroyed one seat and also landed with such force that it created a hole in the concrete. Fortunately, the Yankees were scheduled to play a night game and the incident happened at 3 p.m., so there were no spectators in the area. It occurred five days before the stadium's 75th birthday.

City officials closed the stadium and the Yankees needed to become flexible and resilient with their schedule.

As the stadium was inspected and repaired, the Yankees kept playing in places not named the Bronx. And they kept winning. From Shea Stadium, where the Mets let the Yankees play and where Strawberry homered in his old home and raised the Home Run Apple out of its magic hat, to Detroit, where a series was relocated, to Toronto, the Yankees didn't stumble. They won six of seven games as road warriors to push their streak to 11–1 across a 12-game period. During that time, they outscored opponents, 87–25.

When Yankee Stadium reopened on April 24, Steinbrenner sat with the fans near the Loge Level, Section 22, where the expansion joint had landed, and watched Cone pitch the Yankees to an 8–4 win over the Tigers. The revived Strawberry hammered a titanic two-run homer into the third deck in right field. And, just in case any teams thought the potent Yankees were prone to being intimidated, the Yankees made sure to crush that theory. After Martinez was hit by a pitch in the seventh inning, Mike Stanton plunked Joe Randa in the hip one inning later. If you punch us, we will punch you harder, the Yankees said.

"The thing that stood out for me about that team was just the tenacity," Stanton said. "We just had that killer attitude that we were coming to the ballpark to win. Our mantra was, if we had a game that day, we were going to win that day."

No matter where the Yankees were playing, they kept winning. They were developing a personality, fearless and formidable, dominant and determined. After the Yankees stutter-stepped through the first week of the season, they began showing who they were in emphatic fashion and in 25 different ways. Everyone understood their role. Tim Raines, a future Hall of Famer and a full-time comedian in the clubhouse, was a part-time player. So was Davis, who finished his career with 350 homers. So was Strawberry, who had been one of the most intimidating hitters in baseball and clubbed 335 career homers. Sometimes, Strawberry told Torre to start another player over him if Torre felt that player needed the at-bats.

"The thing I liked about that team is there was no animosity and no jealousy toward each other," Strawberry said. "We all had our roles on that team. I felt like I had a role to play with that club and learning to accept that role was so important. Coming from being a star in the '80s and now I'm playing on a team with a bunch of young stars, I was able to accept that. I accepted fitting in wherever I could fit in."

Sveum, the eagle-eyed teammate, said the Yankees featured "a lineup from hell" that just exhausted pitchers. Oakland's Jimmy Haynes started against the Yankees in the home opener at Yankee Stadium and needed 76 pitches to collect seven outs. The A's lost 17–13 that day. Those high pitch counts were emblematic of what the Yankees did to starters and relievers throughout the season. Relentless. Unforgiving. Merciless. By the time the Yankees had played 27 games, they already had separate winning streaks of eight games, six games, and six games.

Jeter and Posada said they never focused on the Yankees' record and just kept preparing every day and playing every day. Cashman never rested, either. Definitely not in his first month on the job. Heck, definitely not in his first year on the job. Maybe not ever. He was too worried about making mistakes and overworked himself, always wary of what other teams might be doing.

In describing the stress and pressure of being the GM, Cashman said, "It doesn't stop. It never does."

In 1998, neither did the Yankees. They didn't stop. They never did.

CHAPTER 3

Rebel Without a Pause

The pitcher is alone on the mound. In that solitary moment, he decides what pitch he should throw and how he should throw it and where he should throw it. While he is surrounded by his teammates and is being studied by a batter, an umpire, and thousands of fans, he is all by himself. One man, one mound, one stage.

David Wells loved being on that stage and loved being in control of the game. That attention appealed to Wells, the rebel without a pause. Or a filter. Wells liked to work quickly. Get the baseball, get the sign, fire the pitch, and then do it again. He hated wasting time.

Because Wells preferred a quicker pace, he didn't want to shake off a catcher's signs. Wells had to be able to trust his catcher to think along with him so that Wells would see those flashing fingers and execute the pitch. The smoothest type of game for Wells would occur when he never had to shake off any signals, which is precisely what happened when Jorge

Posada caught Wells's perfect game against the Minnesota Twins on May 17.

"Didn't shake him off once," Wells said. "Jorge was perfect that day."

But, before discussing Wells's day of perfection, it is necessary to discuss what happened 11 days earlier. Before perfection, there was imperfection, angst, and anger on a sweltering night in Arlington, Texas. Before Wells, the burly and blustery left-hander, threw the 15th perfect game in major league history, he wandered off the mound in the third inning after nearly blowing a 9–0 lead. He was pissed off at his manager, his manager was pissed off at him, and things were far, very far, from perfect.

It was 94 degrees at game time, which was even steamier than usual for a May night in Arlington and wasn't comfortable for a 240-pound-ish pitcher known as Boomer. There is heat and then there is Texas heat. It's broiling and suffocating. At least it's not 104, Wells thought to himself as he prepared to face a lineup that included Juan González, Iván "Pudge" Rodríguez, and Will Clark. In five months, it would be the same team that Wells would pitch against in Game 1 of the American League Division Series (ALDS). But that assignment was a long way off.

The Yankees, those rampaging Yankees, scored twice in the first inning and added seven more runs in the second to give Wells an early cushion. Wells had retired six of the first seven batters and was cruising with a nine-run lead. This was destined to be a night for Wells and the Yankees to keep cruising. Get the ball, get the sign, throw the pitch, and then do it again. The Yankees had won 21 of their last 23 games. What could go wrong?

It took one pitch for Wells to get the first out in the third, but then everything about the night changed. A lot also changed about Wells's already strained relationship with Manager Joe Torre. The Rangers followed with two singles and a walk to load the bases. After a groundout made it 9–1 and put Wells within one out of escaping, the pitcher and the inning unraveled.

On the mound, Wells kept pulling the shoulders of his sweaty gray jersey toward his neck so that the number 33 on his back was almost colliding with his cap. González scorched a liner that glanced off second baseman Chuck Knoblauch's glove to deliver two runs. Though the ball was smashed, the play was initially ruled an error before being changed to a hit. Posada and pitching coach Mel Stottlemyre visited with Wells and were able to elicit a smile from the pitcher. But that light-heartedness was short-lived as Clark quickly followed with a double. Rodríguez rapped a single past shortstop Derek Jeter to drive in two more. Willie Banks was warming up in the bullpen, which didn't please Wells. Finally, Mike Simms poked a two-run homer off the right field foul pole and, suddenly, it was 9–7. Nine Rangers came to the plate, seven scored and six had hits. Wells wasn't finishing hitters, wasn't focused enough, and seemingly wasn't competing in the way Torre expected him to compete.

Looking irritated in the third base dugout, Torre bolted from his seat, took brisk steps across the dirt and grass, and pointed his right hand toward the bullpen. Wells, who was wandering behind the mound, lifted his arms in disgust, looked toward the outfield, and didn't want to see Torre or speak to Torre. When Torre reached the mound, Wells gave him the baseball as if he was returning an undercooked steak, never made eye contact with his manager, and marched away. It was a show of defiance. It wasn't as defiant as the time Wells chucked the ball down the left field line after Toronto's Cito Gaston removed him from a game in 1991, but it was an unhappy display nonetheless.

"I was going good and I squandered it and Joe got pissed," Wells said. "It's not like I'm trying to give it up. You know? Shit happens. It wasn't cool and Joe and I kind of got into it. But do you know what the thing was? Joe never did that to anybody else. He would never do it to Coney or Pettitte or El Duque or anybody. He had it out for me for some reason."

Reporters noticed the chilly interaction between the manager and the pitcher so, after the Rangers tied the score 13–13 and the Yankees eked out a wild 15–13 win, Torre was asked a lot of questions about Wells. Torre was aggravated with Wells's demeanor and said, "I didn't like the way Wells was walking around on the mound and kicking at it and going slow and just really had bad body language." And then Torre drifted into a sensitive area when he said that Wells "looked like he ran out of gas. Maybe he's out of shape."

Once Wells learned that Torre had mentioned his conditioning as a possible reason for his disappointing outing, he was incensed. There were a lot of buttons to push to infuriate Wells. His weight was one of the hottest buttons of all.

"I was 18–4 that year and you're going to attack me about

my conditioning?" Wells said. "Again, that's just an attack on me because you're pissed off. You don't attack a guy's physique. I'm a big guy."

"And, by the way, I had a weight clause in my contract with Steinbrenner," he continued. "I had to weigh in every week and, if I was over 240, I got fined. And I never got fined that year."

Eager to retaliate with words, Wells told David Cone, his best friend on the team, about his plan to criticize Torre to reporters. Cone, who had been in some toxic clubhouses and some harmonious clubhouses, knew how copasetic this clubhouse was and begged Wells not to rip Torre. Not only was Cone trying to save Wells from digging a deeper hole, he was also trying to save the team from having to deal with the distraction.

"You should set up a meeting with Joe and make sure that Mel is there too," Cone told Wells, knowing that Stottlemyre could act as a mediator, a peacemaker, or, at worst, a referee.

Three days after Wells's lackluster start, he met with Torre and Stottlemyre for about 40 minutes at the Metrodome in Minneapolis. Torre reinforced to Wells that both he and Stottlemyre still had confidence in him and still believed in him. That was a meaningful gesture since Wells had a 5.77 earned run average at the time. Interestingly enough, following the conversation, Wells jogged along the warning track for 15 minutes and did sit-ups in the outfield, things he rarely did in public view. Torre had said he thought Wells needed to lose about five pounds. Wells disagreed. Torre added that Wells's weight "wasn't a big deal unless he's going to have problems in warm weather."

Many times, Torre would shake his head and would respond to something Wells said or did by simply saying, "That's Boomer being Boomer." As the manager, Torre was akin to the father who was trying to nurture 25 sons. Sometimes, one or more of those sons might be rebellious. Wells was that rebel.

"My goal was to try and treat everybody fairly," Torre said. "But I was trying to find the right key to David Wells. I really treated David the only way I knew how. Was it different? At times, it probably was."

While Torre was beloved in the clubhouse by virtually all of his players, Wells didn't attend those fan club meetings. Wells's teammates did.

"For me, Joe was so calming," Cone said. "Just the way he dealt with you and talked to you and treated everybody with such respect. To me, he just seemed like a man who was very comfortable in his own skin and had nothing left to prove. He was very confident and very self-assured. At the same time, he wasn't arrogant about it at all. I don't know how you teach that. He was an MVP and was a great player, but he didn't big league you. He wasn't arrogant in the way he treated players. He treated us with such respect that he demanded respect in return."

Paul O'Neill, another Yankee veteran, added, "Joe was the perfect person for me. He would say the perfect things. As far as his demeanor, I never felt the pressure of whatever was going on upstairs with Mr. Steinbrenner or the front office. I looked at Joe as more of a father figure. And I had a ton of respect for him."

Torre and Wells clashed a lot. Whether it was Wells playing Metallica too loudly in the clubhouse, Wells being late for pregame stretching or a meeting, or Wells leaving the field before batting practice ended, Torre had to repeatedly remind Wells about the team's rules. And Wells wasn't the type who wanted to be reprimanded.

"Joe just tried to manage me and that's the wrong thing to do for a guy who is intense, who wears his emotions on his sleeve, and who isn't going to take shit from anybody," Wells said. "And, to me, that's one of the things I didn't really like."

Forever the nonconformist, Wells didn't want the manager of the team to manage him. Huh? That's not exactly how it's supposed to work.

"That was just Wells's personality," Torre said. "Whatever the reason, he just, I guess, needed the attention. He dared you. He always challenged you."

These days, Torre stressed that he and Wells are cordial to each other and that Wells has joked about how much he aggravated his manager. Still, while Torre searched for the right way to describe his relationship with Wells, he focused on the importance of trust.

"To me, trust is something you have to earn," Torre said. "And I didn't feel that from him. Other than giving him the ball. Man, he would go out there and pitch and he was a tough cookie. He was really tough."

Tough, tenacious, and, at times, callow. When Wells purchased a cap that had been worn by his idol Babe Ruth for $35,000, he mused that he would like to wear it in a game. Without getting permission from Torre, Wells donned the cap with "G. Ruth" stitched inside it for a game in June 1997. Torre made Wells remove it after one inning and fined him $2,500 for violating the uniform policy. Those kinds of incidents exasperated Torre.

"He was just a brat, you know?" Torre said. "He was always pushing the envelope in a stupid way, in my opinion, because the game was more serious to me than maybe it was to him."

But Cone understood Wells's personality better than most and understood how vital it would be for someone to oversee Wells and get the most out of his talented and durable left arm. That's when Cone told Torre, "Let me handle Boomer. I've got him. I will take care of him." A relieved Torre agreed, saying, "Coney was the intermediary for me and Wells because we banged heads a lot. So I trusted Coney on taking care of Wells."

And that's how Coney and Boomer, baseball's Butch Cassidy and the Sundance Kid, became road warriors of a different type. They would travel with the Yankees and, once the airplane landed, they would split from the team and stay in a different hotel. With this strategy, Cone felt Wells would benefit from not being in the bustling team hotel, which was often swarmed by fans and where Wells might have to worry about honoring a curfew or bumping into Torre or a team executive. The plan satisfied the rebel in Wells because it allowed him to snub the authorities and just do his own thing. But, before examining those wild and crazy trips, it's essential to discuss how Wells journeyed through nine innings of perfection.

Wells knew that he shouldn't leave his Upper East Side apartment and go out partying on a Saturday night. Not when he was starting against the Twins the next day. Not with everything that had been swirling around him since his dreadful start in Texas and his clash with Torre. Staying in would have been the prudent thing to do, but Wells has never been prudent.

So Wells ventured out and ended up partying with Jimmy Fallon and other people who were affiliated with *Saturday Night Live*. Season 23 of *SNL* had wrapped a week earlier, but Wells described how he and Fallon and some others drank the night away.

"I really didn't want to drink and Jimmy Fallon started hanging out and we started having drinks and, before you know it, I had probably had a whole bottle of vodka," Wells said. "And we just kept drinking until like 5:30 in the morning."

Fallon validated Wells's story while interviewing Adam Sandler during an episode of *The Tonight Show* in 2022. In recounting the story, Fallon said, "We're hanging out, we're having some drinks, and we're going late." As both realized it was time to go home, Wells said he and Fallon had one of those end-of-the-night conversations that only inebriated folks can have.

"Who is leaving first?" Fallon asked. "You or me?"

Wells said, "Why don't you leave first?"

Fallon responded, "No! You leave first."

Round and round they went, turning an overdue exit into a slurring competition. Finally, Wells said he stumbled away from the bar and had a car service drive him to his apartment.

He slept about two or three hours, woke up, bought a cup of coffee, and drove to Yankee Stadium.

"Man, if I was pulled over, I would have gotten a DUI," Wells said.

Fortunately for Wells and anyone else who was on the road that Sunday, he reached the stadium without any incidents. But, as soon as Wells rumbled into the clubhouse, he had another problem. Cone stared at him, looked away, shook his head, and finally said, "You stink."

"Oh, shit," Wells said. "Is it that bad?"

Cone told Wells the smell of alcohol was wretched and was oozing from his pores.

"If anyone sees you like this, you're not pitching today," Cone said. "Just go hide in the back."

Wells listened to Cone and retreated to the massage room where Rohan Baichu, the Yankees' masseur, was stationed. Still feeling drunk and woozy, Wells flopped on a massage table and asked Baichu to massage his legs to help get him prepared for his start. But Wells said he had to leave the room several times to use the bathroom. The first pitch of the game was creeping closer.

Sticking with his normal routine on an abnormal day, Wells long-tossed in the outfield and it was a chore. When Wells tried plowing through his bullpen session, he was so disoriented that his curveballs bounced several feet in front of the plate and two fastballs sailed over the bullpen wall.

"Looking great," Stottlemyre said.

Wells shot back, "I'm doing shitty. Don't patronize me."

Realizing that he was probably still drunk and that it wasn't too smart to tell the pitching coach how sloppy he looked and how sluggish he felt, Wells closed his mouth—and maybe even closed his eyes—and hoped for the best. And that's what Wells found in front of 49,820 fans who came to the stadium to get a Beanie Baby and went home with much more.

With the top two buttons of his pinstriped jersey undone and a gray T-shirt underneath, Wells wobbled to the mound. He had no idea what to expect, but after that first fastball pierced through the strike zone with solid velocity, Wells stood a bit steadier. He zoomed through the first inning on nine pitches.

Wells had another 1-2-3 inning in the second, which included striking out Ron Coomer, who had been 8 for 13 against him in his career. He was crawling through the afternoon. Crawling became walking when Wells struck out the side in the third, one on a curve, one on a fastball, and one on a changeup. Some fans scribbled K's on sheets of paper and taped them in front of their seats.

Somewhere in the New York area, Fallon had slept off his night of drinking before awakening to a shocking sight.

"It's gotta be one o'clock or 1:30 the next day," Fallon explained. "I turn on the TV, and David Wells is pitching."

At first, Fallon thought he was watching an encore version of another classic Wells game. But, very quickly, Fallon realized the man who was drinking with him until 5:30 a.m. was pitching a perfect game.

"It's the craziest thing in the world to see that thing," Fallon told Sandler on his show.

Sandler screamed, "He's a mad man!"

The mad man rolled into the fourth inning and fell behind Matt Lawton with a 3–0 count, the first threat to perfection. But he got Lawton to pop out on a 3–1 pitch. Wells retired the next two batters to finish another clean inning. Twelve Twins had batted and 12 had been retired and now Wells said, "I was finally feeling like myself."

More aware and more vibrant than he had been all afternoon, Wells deftly mixed his fastball, his cutter, and his looping curve to strike out two in the fifth and two more in the sixth. The Twins hadn't really come close to collecting a hit. Wells fell behind 2–0 on Lawton to start the seventh, but Lawton did him a favor by swinging at a pitch that was a ball and lifting it to center. After a groundout, Paul Molitor, an aggressive batter who would finish his career with 3,319 hits, stared at a 3–2 fastball for strike three. Maybe Tim McClelland, the plate umpire, was feeling the moment because the pitch was probably a bit outside. No matter. Wells had seven perfect innings, orchestrated by Posada.

"He didn't like to shake off signs," Posada said. "When I put signs down that day, he threw the pitches exactly where I wanted them. He was unbelievable."

Wells said he was "a lonely man that day" because his teammates adhered to the baseball superstition of not speaking to a pitcher who is throwing a no-hitter, or a perfect game. But Wells is always talkative and jumpy and he wanted to have some conversation. When Wells sat beside Tino Martinez, Martinez jumped off the bench as if he had been electrocuted and moved to another spot in the dugout.

Finally, Cone, sensing how anxious Wells seemed, said, "I think it's time to break out the knuckleball."

"What?" Wells said. "I don't have a knuckleball."

Cone reminded Wells how they played catch every day and that Wells did dabble with a knuckleball. As Wells bickered with Cone about whether or not he had a useful knuckleball, he realized that Cone "was just trying to take the pressure off me." Since Wells laughed, it must have worked.

In the eighth, Jeter bobbled a grounder before recovering to get the first out of the inning. Coomer hit a bullet to second, but Knoblauch knocked it down and coolly notched the out at first. A pop-up to first ended the inning. Wells was three outs away.

In the bottom of the eighth, Wells sat quietly in the dugout, stretching his neck, shaking his head, and swinging his shoulders from side to side to stay loose. He wore a Yankee jacket, but still had a white towel wrapped around his left arm. Wells looked impatient. He was ready to pitch. As soon as Martinez popped out to end the inning, Wells removed the jacket, grabbed his glove, and barged out of the dugout.

With the excitable fans standing and clapping and hoping for history, Wells continued to pump strikes, just as he had done all day. It took seven pitches for Wells to retire Jon Shave on a pop fly to right field and then he whiffed Javier Valentín on a nifty curveball in the dirt. He was one out away. The batter was Pat Meares, an infielder who was 5 for 23 against Wells in his career, including going hitless in his last 11 at bats.

One more out to perfection for Boomer. Was this a dream? How could Wells, who was about 10 hours removed from his last gulp of vodka, be within one out of a feat that only 14 pitchers had ever accomplished? How had this happened? They were great questions and they might have been unanswerable questions. In the dugout, a nervous Cone wore sunglasses and pulled his jacket up so high on his chin that his head was barely visible. He looked like an antsy turtle.

On the second pitch of the at-bat, Wells threw an outside fastball and Meares lifted a lazy fly ball down the right field line. Wells quickly turned to watch the flight of the ball, backpedaling off the mound and starting to smile as he waited for O'Neill to catch it. When O'Neill snared it at 4:16 p.m., Wells pumped his fist twice and was soon engulfed by his teammates in front of the mound. Backup infielder Luis Sojo was the first player to sprint out of the dugout and embrace Wells, who hugged teammate after teammate. The warmest hug was shared with Posada, his copilot to perfection.

Weight wasn't a problem as Darryl Strawberry, Bernie Williams, and Banks hoisted Wells on their shoulders like a king and carried him to the first base dugout. A beaming Wells sat on the blue bench, breathing heavily and giving more high fives to teammates after his 11-strikeout masterpiece. Cone nudged Wells and suggested he return to the field for a curtain call, which Wells did. The day didn't start perfectly, but it ended that way.

"We had a great game plan against Minnesota," Posada said. "They threw a lot of righty batters against David and he pitched well against righties because he had a great cutter. It made his fastball even better. And his curveball was just unbelievable that day. He was snapping it off and he had great control with it and they weren't recognizing it. His curve was probably the reason why he threw a perfect game."

Wells called Posada his all-time favorite catcher because of his ability to read Wells's mind and the two share an impenetrable bond. As a pitcher who loathed the thought of walking hitters, Wells told Posada he typically wanted to throw sinkers when he was behind in the count to get strikes or induce contact. Other than that advice, Wells trusted Posada to read what the hitters were doing at the plate and to assess how Wells's pitches were reacting and to call the next pitch.

"To have Jorge think with me made me so much better," Wells said. "I didn't have to think when I was out there. He did the thinking for me. On that day, he called a great game. When people ask me the best catcher I ever threw to, I say, 'Hands down, it was Jorge.'"

One perfect day doesn't mean every subsequent day was blissful. Posada was as passionate and as intense as any player I ever covered, a player who was never hesitant to tell a pitcher how he felt about a disappointing pitch or an awful outing. As Posada's stature and playing time increased, he became as much of a leader as any Yankee. And, if he felt the need to get loud and demonstrative with his perfect game pitcher, he would.

The afterglow of the 1998 season didn't last too long for Wells. He was bitter and angry when the Yankees made a bold move by trading him, Graeme Lloyd, and Homer Bush to the Toronto Blue Jays for Roger Clemens in the spring of 1999. Cone tried to console Wells, but there was no consoling a player who loved being a Yankee.

But, when we fast-forward to the 2003 season, Wells was a Yankee again and was now teammates with Clemens. That's quite a dynamic duo in the rotation, right? Yes, it was. But not on successive days against the White Sox in late August. Clemens was blitzed for nine earned runs and didn't last through the fifth inning in a 13–2 drubbing on August 26. One day later, Wells allowed 10 earned runs in five and a third innings in an 11–2 rout. Posada caught both games and he was perturbed with the horrible results. The performance was something Posada addressed with Wells.

"And we were in the clubhouse, him and I, and he basically got in my face," Wells said. "I don't know if I pushed him into the pillar and got in his face too. But I said, 'If you put different fingers down, maybe it would have been a different story.'"

Despite Wells's cheap shot of a remark, he actually appreciated the fact that Posada challenged him.

"I saw how frustrated Jorge was," Wells said. "We had a bad series and Jorge happened to be right there in the middle of it. He wasn't happy about it and he wanted better out of us."

After Wells's perfecto, he received a congratulatory call from Don Larsen, the only other Yankee to pitch a perfect game to that point. Larsen did it against the Brooklyn Dodgers in Game 5 of the 1956 World Series and, in an eerie and unbelievable coincidence, he and Wells had both graduated from Point Loma High School in San Diego. Larsen received his diploma in 1947 and Wells secured his 45 years later. Fourteen months after Wells followed Larsen in perfection, Cone joined both of them by pitching a perfect game on July 18, 1999.

It had been a topsy-turvy 12 days for Wells. He went

from nearly blowing a 9–0 lead and arguing with his manager to doing something extraordinary. Ken Singleton, a former major leaguer with more than 2,000 hits and one of the broadcasters for the perfect game, summed up Wells's recent adventures neatly when he said, "When you go back a couple of starts, David Wells was mad at the world. A few starts later, they carry him off the field."

What is the moral to Wells's story from being so hungover that his skull rattled to being absolutely perfect?

"It was a stupid thing to do," Wells said. "I just got lucky. That's the only way to look at it. It was pure luck and then getting locked in. My bullpen was so bad and my first pitch of the game was right down the middle at 93 or 94. I was like, 'Wow, where did that come from?' I kind of keyed off that. I just threw to the glove."

He paused and added, "Well, what I could see of the glove."

Whether there was a cause and effect between Torre criticizing Wells and Wells getting angry and Cone getting involved, we will never know. But there had to be some connection between those events. Even if Torre's criticism emboldened Wells to simply prove his manager wrong, he was a much more competitive pitcher on a day where he felt queasy and it would have been easy for him to fade. He didn't. He fought. For one afternoon, he was perfect.

With the euphoria of Wells's perfect game still hovering over the Yankees, they played the Orioles two days later. Wells was giddy and was still being praised for his amazing afternoon of perfection. But baseball teams play almost every day and story lines can change quickly. And, as the Yankees soon learned, one way to shift the attention from a perfect pitching performance is with a cowardly pitching performance that leads to a huge brawl.

Ladies and gentleman, let me introduce Armando Benítez.

It wasn't even June and the Orioles already trailed the first place Yankees by a whopping 11 games, so they desperately needed to play well at Yankee Stadium. Benítez was clinging to a one-run lead with two outs in the eighth inning when Williams demolished a splitter and sent it into the right field upper deck for a three-run homer. The Yankees led, 7–5.

Showing his frustration and his immaturity, Benítez's next pitch was a fastball that drilled Martinez between the 2 and the 4 on his back. Everyone with a pulse knew Benítez had hit Martinez intentionally and plate umpire Drew Coble immediately ejected Benítez from the game. But the Yankees didn't care about the ejection. They cared about retribution. Especially when Benítez dropped his glove and motioned with his fingertips for them to come toward him.

The imposing Strawberry, acting as the Yankees' six-foot-six security guard, rushed out of the first base dugout with his hands out. But he was stopped by some Orioles. As the other Yankees dashed onto the field, they were the aggressors and forced Benítez and the Orioles back toward the third baseline. Relievers Graeme Lloyd and Jeff Nelson hustled in from the bullpen, maneuvered around the crowd of players, and got close enough to take some wayward swings at Benítez, who kept backing up closer to his own dugout.

"We went after them," said Posada. "And it was everybody on our team who did that. We were on top of their dugout. We came to them. There were a lot of things that happened in that incident that showed you we weren't backing down."

As the players grabbed each other and a bunch of near scuffles seemed poised to erupt, the Yankees kept targeting Benítez, dozens of sets of eyes following one man. For a few seconds, Benítez and Scott Brosius stood toe to toe like boxers and looked as if they might square off, but no punches were thrown. And then Strawberry barreled into Benítez and shoved him into the dugout. Cone wasn't surprised by Strawberry's persistence.

"Straw was right in the middle of that fight," Cone said. "He was kind of the enforcer. He was the kind of guy who really believed in protecting his teammates. He had a real strong reputation for that. I certainly learned that from him."

Victimized by Benítez's petty action, Martinez desperately tried to get close enough to retaliate. But Martinez was restrained by B. J. Surhoff and some other Orioles. Martinez's eyes were angry and ablaze, staring in Benítez's direction. There were more than 50 Orioles and Yankees pushing, shoving, and screaming around the Orioles' dugout. Half of them wanted to destroy Benítez and the other half were annoyed with their reckless pitcher.

"The Orioles' players have to be embarrassed by what Benítez did," said Jim Kaat, a broadcaster who won 288 games,

16 Gold Gloves, and was enshrined into the Baseball Hall of Fame in 2022. "Totally classless."

Nelson inched close enough to Benítez to unleash a punch, but, before he could, it was Benítez who flicked two punches. With Benítez surrounded by some Orioles and perched near the top step of the dugout, Strawberry finally spotted another opening. Like a defensive back attacking a quarterback from the blind side, Strawberry rumbled in from Benítez's left side and struck him in the face. Both players tumbled into the dugout and another 15 or 20 bodies fell in with them. Alan Mills connected with a right hand to Strawberry's face and bloodied Strawberry's mouth. Manager Joe Torre stood inches away from Strawberry and pleaded with him to leave the Orioles' dugout and then Torre helped escort Strawberry back to the Yankees' dugout.

"I didn't want my teammates to get hurt or get suspended just because of me," Martinez said. "But when they all went out there at one time and guys were coming in from the bullpen and guys were flying out of the dugout, it was chaos."

"After it was all said and done, I think we proved to other teams that, hey, we might be a bunch of nice guys who play the game the right way day in and day out, but, like Darryl Strawberry said, 'Don't mess with us.' Don't treat us the wrong way because we will respond," Martinez said.

Principal owner George Steinbrenner, who was visibly shaken as he spoke with reporters outside the Yankee clubhouse, chastised Benítez and said that he "could really kill a guy with the way he threw that ball." Steinbrenner was right. And when Steinbrenner, always a fighter, was asked what he felt about his team, he said, "How can you feel? We took it right to them. I feel very proud of them. All of them."

The Yankees had galvanized. They were already a streaking team, a talented team that had confidence and swagger. But Benítez roused something within the Yankees and helped a spirited team become even closer.

"What we showed is that we had each other's back," Posada said. "We came out and we helped our brother, our teammate, our partner. We were not going to take that shit from anyone. When that happens, it's a type of brotherhood that develops. I think we showed that we had it that night. I think that made us closer than we were. That was probably one of the key moments of the year."

Martinez, the target, agreed.

"It was a crazy, crazy brawl," said Martinez. "We already had a good team before that. After that, it definitely felt like we knew we had each other's backs, no matter. No matter who was out there on the mound and no matter which one of our guys got hit by a pitch, we were going to take care of everybody on our team."

The game resumed with Tim Raines batting for the Yankees and he promptly hit Bobby Muñoz's first pitch for a homer. It was as symbolic and as powerful a gesture as a team could provide on a baseball field. One day after Benítez's reckless behavior, he received an eight-game suspension. Strawberry and Lloyd were each suspended three games and Nelson and Mills were suspended two games.

To this day, Martinez has no idea why Benítez threw at him because he's never spoken with Benítez. During the brawl,

Martinez held up two fingers to Benítez while saying, "This is the second time." Indeed, it was. On June 7, 1995, Seattle's Edgar Martinez belted a grand slam off Benítez. He followed that by plunking the next batter: Tino Martinez. And the Orioles promptly sent Benítez to the minor leagues.

"I would call it a reckless move," said Martinez, who went 18 for 100 after being hit on the right shoulder blade. "I have no idea what he was thinking."

Thirteen months after hitting Martinez, Benítez, who was now with the Mets, said he regretted the pitch. But Benítez also tried to claim that he was simply throwing inside. No one would ever believe that. Benítez's own teammates criticized his actions and the Orioles didn't use him against the Yankees for the rest of the 1998 season. Interestingly, Benítez revealed that he sent Martinez a letter of apology three days after the incident. He never found out if Martinez received it. When Martinez was asked about the letter, he didn't want to discuss it and said, "Why is that important?"

Maybe it was or maybe it wasn't. What was important to the Yankees is that they were punched and they punched back, harder and harder. They bonded even more as a team on that brawling night in the Bronx.

While all 25 Yankees were bonding during that special season, there were two Yankees in particular whose bond was a bit stronger than most. Cone and Wells were pitching buddies, drinking buddies, and traveling buddies, an insightful right-hander with a splitter and a slider and a bellowing left-hander with a sinker and a curve. And they were doing things their way.

When Wells pitched for the 1996 Orioles, he was intrigued by how Cal Ripken Jr. didn't typically stay at the team hotel on road trips because he wanted to find some serenity. Ripken, who set a record by playing in 2,632 consecutive games, was a superstar and a future Hall of Fame player, so he would get besieged by autograph seekers in and around the hotel. To avoid that attention, Ripken and Brady Anderson usually would stay in a separate hotel.

Impressed with Ripken's road strategy and always interested in pushing back against authority, Wells mentioned the idea to Cone. Cone liked the idea, too, so they made their own arrangements in a few cities in 1997. But, when Wells and Torre were squabbling in early May, Cone realized that getting Wells away from the team hotel and away from any discipline and any scrutiny was the smartest approach. Cone had told Torre, "Let me have Boomer. I will keep him out of jail," and volunteered to be Wells's friend and chaperone of sorts. One of the ways Cone did that was by locating a five-star hotel, making the reservations, and having a party for two. Or more.

"We just kept the routine going all year," Cone said. "And Boomer found his friend and I grew to love the guy. I knew him from '92 when we were with the Blue Jays and I liked him. But we all know Boomer. Boomer was kind of crazy. He was the guy who needed the pat on the back. Some guys need a kick in the butt. Some need a pat on the back. Boomer needed a friend. He needed someone to believe in him."

Cone was that someone. Wells was the son of a woman named Eugenia Ann who was nicknamed "Attitude Annie" and who dated a chapter president of the Hells Angels Motorcycle Club in San Diego. Naturally, her son had a rebellious side. Cone understood that about his friend and realized that Wells would likely flourish if he had the chance to be himself.

Whether it was a Ritz Carlton or a Four Seasons or another luxury hotel, Cone tried to book suites that had two bedrooms and a common area and enabled Wells and him to invite friends to hang out. Wells was buddies with Lars Ulrich from Metallica and Geddy Lee from Rush and a roster of other musicians, band managers, and roadies and, on any given night, there was a party going on in their perfect suite. Teammates had an open invitation.

"We let everybody know," Cone said, "except management."

Now free from whatever limitations he might have felt at a team hotel, Wells said, "We could just be ourselves and not look over our shoulder."

Cone stressed that his arrangement with Wells wasn't about debauchery or excess, although there were some examples of both. He said it was about "bonding" and becoming close as teammates and about thriving too.

And the policy worked for both of them. From the day of Wells's perfect game until the end of the season, Cone and Wells were two of the best pitchers in the major leagues. Wells was 14–3 with a 2.93 ERA and 123 strikeouts and 15 walks in 162⅔ innings, while Cone was 15–6 with a 2.88 ERA and 171 strikeouts and 46 walks in 168⅔ innings. Clemens won the American League Cy Young Award that season, Pedro Martínez finished second and Wells and Cone, two road buddies, finished third and fourth. It was impossible to argue with their approach.

"Wells took off and he dragged me along with him," Cone said. "I thought it was a great thing. I ended up growing fond of him and understanding him. We both picked each other up. We had a one-two punch going that year."

In this distinct environment, Wells did flourish. The numbers show it.

"We went out every night before Coney pitched or before I pitched," Wells said. "Well, 90 percent of the time we went out. But we didn't go out and get annihilated. We just went out and had a few pops. It was something that just became like a tradition. And it worked."

And what became of the Torre-Wells relationship?

"Torre left him alone," Cone said. "It became easier to just leave him alone. He was a lights-out pitcher."

Again, it's fairly uncommon for major league players to stay apart from the team during road trips. When I asked Torre how comfortable he was with letting Cone and Wells do that, he said, "Well, let's put it this way: I didn't necessarily trust Wells, but I trusted Coney."

How stealthy were Cone and Wells? Even though Cone said that they invited teammates to their road sanctuary, Bush, a rookie who was with the Yankees for the entire season, was startled when he heard what Cone and Wells did. Not only was Bush startled, he was in awe.

"That's some high-level thinking on Coney's part," Bush said. "Sometimes, you have to find the wrong way to do the right thing."

The Cone-Wells friendship prospered even after they had a clubhouse fight in June 1997. Actually, it was an accidental one-punch fight. On a hot and humid night in Miami, Wells labored through a five-run first inning against the Marlins. Gary Sheffield cracked a grand slam, but Wells was especially annoyed by plate umpire Greg Bonin's strike zone.

When Wells batted in the top of the second, he complained to Bonin and used a few choice words and was immediately ejected. It was an incredibly selfish move by a starting pitcher. The Yankees had lost to the Marlins, 2–1, in 12 innings the night before, a game in which Cone tossed nine innings. Now Wells's nonsense had put the bullpen in position to have to cover eight innings.

Cone never invited confrontations with teammates, but he didn't shy away from them, either. If a teammate did something reckless that could hurt the team, Cone would definitely let him know about it. And Wells's actions did hurt the team. As Wells left the dugout and returned to the clubhouse, Cone followed him and said, "Dude, what the heck was that?" Wells began complaining about Bonin and didn't seem to sense the gravity of the situation so Cone interjected and said, "You just hung us out to dry. Now we have to clear out our whole bullpen to cover for you. You quit on us." Wells kept dropping f-bombs and moved in Cone's direction. As Wells did that, Cone said he tried to avoid Wells and stuck out his right hand and inadvertently punched his teammate in the mouth. It wasn't much of a punch. It wasn't meant to incite anything physical. But Cone did want his words, not necessarily the punch, to resonate. "If you want to fight, we'll fight, but remember, you quit on us tonight," Cone repeated.

And the words did sink in. Cone said Wells looked sheepish and finally began to realize how selfish his actions had been. The game was postponed by rain soon after Wells's ejection, but the Yankees still needed to use 10 pitchers in a doubleheader the next day. After the fight that wasn't much of a physical fight, Cone and Wells continued their discussion by sharing some drinks in a Miami bar. Playing both friend, teammate, and psychologist, Cone told Wells how important he was to the team.

"You can't let something like that happen," Cone told Wells. "You're better than that. We need you to be a leader out there, not someone who puts the team in a bind."

Slowly, from one drink to the next (and the next), Wells understood that Cone was right. Wells later spoke to reporters and apologized for his actions. And Cone considered that night a breakthrough in the friendship between the two pitchers, a night where a thoughtless act led to a punch and some wisdom. But Cone said Wells's behavior made his already tenuous relationship with Torre even more fragile. That's another reason why Cone knew it was good to stow Wells away on the road.

"I think the culmination of that is, even though he and I got over it that night, he and Torre's relationship really deteriorated after that," Cone said.

Torre and Wells learned to coexist in 1998 and, again, Cone and Wells thrived together. Cone tossed seven shutout innings in his final start of the season to defeat Tampa Bay and notch his 20th win on his third attempt. As Cone watched the ninth inning from the players' lounge in the clubhouse, he was elated when Mariano Rivera pitched a clean ninth to finalize the win. But, as satisfied as Cone was in securing his 20th, he didn't expect to have teammates who were even happier.

And, when catcher Joe Girardi left the field and located Cone in the clubhouse, he handed him the game ball and said, "I wanted that bad." Cone was overwhelmed. He cried. Girardi cried too. Steinbrenner had a bottle of Korbel champagne sent to Cone with the message, "Congratulations from the Boss. Keep up the good work." With Cone's 20th in 1998, the 35-year-old had set a record for the longest stretch between 20-victory seasons since he had also won 20 with the Mets in 1988. Stottlemyre was his pitching coach in both milestone seasons. Kaat had held the previous record with 20-win campaigns separated by eight seasons.

"I'm not even sure what that record means," Cone said. "It's based off a won-loss record. I guess doing it 10 years apart is something to be proud of. To still be in the position to do something like that 10 years later is pretty cool."

Meanwhile, Wells went from bickering with Torre in May to being named Torre's number one postseason starter. And Wells deserved the nod. One year earlier, Wells had struggled so mightily that Torre waited until late September before revealing Wells's status for the postseason (the Game 3 starter in the Division Series against Cleveland). But, whatever Wells had done in the past to frustrate Torre, he had earned the first start for a historic team. Cone said he repeatedly thanks Wells for "what he did in 1998. He won all four of his starts in the playoffs. He's a major reason we got that ring."

How calm was Wells against the Rangers? Before facing the second batter, he paused and waved to the boisterous fans who chanted his name from the bleachers. He breezed through eight scoreless innings in a 2–0 win, even assuring Torre during a late mound visit that he could handle Roberto Kelly. And Wells wasn't lying as he struck out Kelly as the potential tying run.

"He's a battler now," Torre said. "He finds a way to stay in the game. He doesn't quit. He's changed that completely."

A delirious Wells said, "I'm glad he stuck with me and showed faith in me. That means a lot."

Following Wells's performance, a headline in the *New York Times* read, "No Longer a Problem, Boomer Is the Solution." It was a dramatic turnaround for a pitcher who was more of a problem for Torre than a solution in early May. Because Wells is Wells, he did remind everyone that Torre had doubted him in 1997. Wells also called himself a fighter and a headbanger too. Yes, a headbanger.

"I'm a headbanger," Wells said. "I spoke to Eddie Van Halen last night and told him to wear the jersey I gave him. Just wear it for the vibes, man. The guy can shred a guitar. Send me the vibes, man."

The vibes around the 1998 Yankees were positive, all positive. After a rewarding and adventurous regular season, Cone was relieved and proud to have won his 20th game while

Wells was stoked and proud to have won the ALDS opener. There was only one lingering issue for Butch and Sundance to address. With the Yankees leaving the Bronx for some postseason games, it was time to stay in the team hotel again.

CHAPTER 4

International Man of Mystery

The mystery man was tall and lean and he was smiling, perpetually smiling. His life had dramatically changed when he courageously left Cuba in a fishing boat and it was about to change again. Every day featured more changes, more smiles, and more glimpses of the pitcher known as El Duque.

This was the scene on a sunny spring training day where Orlando "El Duque" Hernández first pitched in front of the Yankees. After fleeing Cuba on the day after Christmas in 1997, he took a dangerous and circuitous route to signing a four-year, $6.6 million contract with the Yankees. Now Hernández was finally on a mound in Tampa in late March, surrounded by curious Yankee coaches and executives who were eager to see the mystery man pitch.

He tossed a baseball softly and confidently, the ball snapping off his fingertips and popping into the catcher's mitt. There was an ease and a swagger about El Duque, a recognition that all eyes were on him and a realization that he adored the attention. After 14 miserable months without playing baseball in Cuba and three more months of finding his next baseball team, he was finally pitching again.

So began the El Duque show—when he pitched from a windup and unveiled a funky motion that was different from any that the attendees had ever seen. Hernández's eyes looked menacing as he held his glove in front of his face, but it was his limber and acrobatic leg kick that made him so distinctive. He lifted his left leg and it climbed higher and higher, his knee almost brushing his chin, and then he peered to the side before reconnecting with the target and powering forward to fire a pitch. It was athletic. It was balletic. It was gorgeous. Who was this mystery man?

"He showed up for this bullpen session in Tampa and he just had this presence about him like he was Michael Jordan," said General Manager Brian Cashman. "There was something projecting from him, a presence that you could feel. It was greatness. He wasn't cocky, but there was something about him."

There was something so special about Hernández that Cashman compared him to Jordan, one of the most famous athletes on the planet and a man who was known to be ultra-confident and ultracompetitive. Yes, that's who Cashman thought of when he first watched the mystery man with no major league innings on his résumé.

"I feel like when you're around successful people, they emit an aura about them," Cashman said. "And before El Duque knew what he could do around here, he was emitting that aura. He had a presence."

International Man of Mystery

A presence. A major presence. Cashman wasn't alone in instantly noticing El Duque's confidence and his talents. It was evident that Hernández, who was thrilled to be pitching again and thrilled to be a Yankee, had charisma. I think he was thrilled to be showing off too. He had been the king of the mound in Cuba, a baseball-obsessed country where he had a gaudy 129–47 record for Havana's Industriales, who are Cuba's version of the Yankees.

After Liván, his half brother, defected in 1995, El Duque was banished from the Cuban National team for life in October 1996. Obviously, if one Hernández brother had left the country to pitch in the major leagues, Cuban authorities believed the other brother might try to do the same thing. Since Liván had defected while the Cuban team was playing in Mexico, the Cubans figured there was much less of a chance of El Duque defecting if he wasn't playing baseball and wasn't allowed to leave the island.

But, now as a Yankee, Hernández was free and he was superb. With his Yankees cap pulled down tight to his brow and his blue stirrups hiked up to his knee, El Duque made his major league debut before a modest crowd of 27,291 on June 3. He pitched seven innings in a 7–1 victory over the Tampa Bay Devil Rays at Yankee Stadium, a day that was as meaningful and as humbling as any day in Hernández's life. The locomotive known as the Yankees were 40–13 after that win and weren't in need of any extra help, but El Duque, the cagey and clever pitcher, made a great team even better. The starters had a 4.14 ERA before Hernández arrived and a 3.48 ERA, including the playoffs, after he became a Yankee.

How could El Duque pitch so effectively with a leg kick that would make a Rockette proud? How many arm angles did he use? How many pitches did he throw? Was he a pitching magician? The questions hovered over Hernández and he answered them all emphatically while going 12–4 with a 3.13 earned run average and winning the Yankees' most important game of the postseason in the American League Championship Series. He was immune to pressure, which was understandable for a pitcher who had bolted from Cuba in a boat and with a lot of hope.

"I don't think anybody has written the right movie script for this guy," said catcher Jorge Posada. "There's no way to really tell his story and what he had to go through to get here and pitch for the Yankees. That's just a movie waiting to happen. It was unbelievable."

Well, this is Hernández's story, which has been told and revised and told again. On a still morning in Cuba, hours after families had celebrated the first legal Christmas in the country in 28 years, Hernández and Noris Bosch, the girlfriend who became his wife, and six others waded into the water at Conuco Cay. They climbed onto a boat and started their surreptitious departure from Cuba. According to the meticulously reported *The Duke of Havana*, El Duque complained about the boat and called it "a piece of shit." But Bosch bluntly said, "We've made our decision. Better to drown than to turn back now."

Cuba had been El Duque's home and the place where he had risen to stardom, but it was also the place that oppressed him and silenced him. He had been one of the most well-known

Cubans as an accomplished and stylish pitcher who threw his fastball in the low 90s and also had a variety of breaking pitches, but he was now working at a psychiatric hospital for $9 a month. He longed to hold a baseball, throw a baseball, and be a pitcher again.

The trip was treacherous because the group was so tense about being spotted, stopped, and punished. Hernández's boat was described as "a 20-foot sailboat made of scraps" and as a 17-foot raft (by me) in the *Times*. Additionally, there had been reports about the boat nearly sinking in stormy and shark-infested waters. But those details were erroneous. After the 1998 season, *Sports Illustrated* interviewed three passengers who traveled with El Duque and they explained how they were in a 20-foot wooden fishing boat with a six-cylinder engine. The other passengers also said the boat didn't take on any water, the weather was perfect, and they didn't encounter any sharks. Whatever the type of boat, it was still a risky and unnerving trip. Hernández and several others spent the first four hours of the trip crowded inside the sweaty cabin of the boat.

After about 10 hours, the group landed on Anguilla Cay, a small island that belongs to the Bahamas. A second boat that was supposed to meet the group and take them to Miami never arrived, which resulted in them being stranded on the island for four days. The travelers weren't expecting to be marooned and only brought two cans of Spam, 10 pounds of sugar, and several gallons of water, so they survived on those sparse items and some seaweed and conch. According to *The Duke of Havana*, El Duque was so unprepared for the possibility of an extended journey that he had only a pack of cigarettes. A United States Coast Guard helicopter finally saw El Duque and his group, rescued them, and brought them to an immigration center in the Bahamas.

Within hours, Joe Cubas, a Cuban American sports agent, arrived to counsel Hernández. While Hernández was offered a visa by the United States, he was savvy enough to instead seek political asylum and establish residency in Costa Rica. Cubas, who was known as "El Gordo" or "The Fat Man" and who had helped Liván and other Cubans defect, educated El Duque on Major League Baseball's rules and the importance of being a free agent. If Hernández had accepted the U.S. visa, he would have had to participate in the amateur draft. In that scenario, El Duque would have been chosen by one team and would have had to negotiate a contract with that team. By journeying to Costa Rica, Hernández became a free agent and could be courted by any of the 30 teams. It was the first of many smart decisions Hernández would make. Cubas had secured a $4.5 million deal from the Marlins for Liván and he was committed to getting a more lucrative contract for El Duque, who had been the more successful pitcher.

As Hernández was being scrutinized by teams, there was evidence that he was 32 years old, based on the birth date listed on an old baseball card. But El Duque insisted he was 28. Cashman joked that the Yankees would consider Hernández 28 if they signed him and 32 if another team signed him. Well, after auditioning for 60 scouts in Costa Rica, the 28-year-old Hernández (wink, wink) became a Yankee.

Even after Hernández's memorable audition in March, the

Yankees planned to be methodical about promoting him to the majors. The Yankees realized they probably rushed Japanese pitcher Hideki Irabu to the big leagues after he made only eight minor league starts in 1997 and then struggled and ended up with a 7.09 ERA in the majors. They didn't want to make the same mistake with Hernández. Instead, they wanted Hernández, who hadn't pitched in a game since his banishment in Cuba, to pitch in the minor leagues and get adjusted to being in the United States. But El Duque fast-tracked himself. He was 7–1 with a 3.33 ERA and 74 strikeouts in 51⅓ innings in the minors, pushing himself closer and closer to the majors.

The El Duque story was filled with suspense and drama and excitement and, as Posada noted, felt like a movie script playing out in real time. Even Hernández's major league debut had an interesting twist to it. El Duque only started against Tampa Bay on June 3 because David Cone, who was supposed to pitch, was bitten on his index finger by his mother's Jack Russell terrier. Cone said Veronica, the terrier, had teeth as "sharp as hypodermic needles." Suddenly, El Duque was starting for the New York Yankees.

"George Steinbrenner never believed that story," Cone said. "Nobody believed it. George used to say, 'Where were you? A dog bite? So what really happened?' But it was true."

It was the old dog-bites-man-and-helps-create-a-pitching-legend story because, once Hernández made it to the mound at Yankee Stadium, he never left. In El Duque's victorious debut, some fans waved Cuban flags and watched the Cuban maestro make himself at home in the Bronx. When El Duque saw the flags of his homeland, he said, "I couldn't hold back my tears. And I said to myself, 'OK. What are you waiting for? Go out and do a good job.'" In a postgame interview, Hernández was asked what message he might send to Castro and he told the MSG Network, "I would not say anything to him because I would not waste my time standing in front of him."

In a season filled with memory after memory, that first game is still El Duque's favorite recollection because it was the beginning of his new life. As he discussed it 25 years later, he was moved by how much that day meant to him.

"It seems like everything that year was good to me because it was all new," said Hernández. "For two years, I went without playing baseball. Everyone knows the cause of that. And then I had the opportunity to play in the major leagues and meet so many good players. Everything was so good for me. But, if you're looking for special things, I would say June 3, 1998, was very, very special."

Before the Devil Rays faced the mystery man on that day, John Flaherty, one of their catchers, said the team's scouting report on Hernández detailed a decent fastball and a sweeping slider. But Flaherty soon realized the assessment didn't come close to describing El Duque as a pitcher.

"Our reports didn't say anything about how well he hid the baseball or how his leg kick impacted your timing or how his fastball played up because of the breaking pitches he threw and everything he did," Flaherty said. "If you were grading him on just his stuff, it would be at the bottom end. But it was everything about him that made him so special."

Six days after Hernández's debut, it was another rewarding day as he pitched a complete game four-hitter in an 11–1 win over the Montreal Expos. The Yankees were impressed, beyond impressed, with their mystery man. They knew Hernández was good, but they didn't know he was THIS good. El Duque's performances forced the Yankees to alter their plans. The Yankees had said El Duque was likely to return to the minors, but they had no choice but to keep Hernández in the rotation and relegate the versatile Ramiro Mendoza to the bullpen. This development coincided with what El Duque always had prophesied.

"I told one of our minor league coaches, 'If they bring me to the big leagues, I'm never going back to the minors,'" Hernández said.

Covering El Duque in his early days with the Yankees was highly entertaining, a different show every time he took the baseball. He was just different. Even the way he prepared before games was different. Before El Duque ever picked up a ball and long-tossed it across the outfield, he readied himself in the way a long-distance runner might prepare. He did wind sprints, leg lifts, arm circles, and other calisthenics. When Hernández did pick up a ball to long-toss, he would use a bigger softball before switching to a baseball. El Duque, who was as fit as anyone on the roster, made other pitchers look like weekend warriors.

Most major league pitchers don't speak to reporters before their starts, but Hernández was different in that respect too. Hernández didn't know that unwritten rule about declining pre-game interviews or he didn't care about it or he was just emulating Cone, his talkative buddy, because El Duque often engaged with the media leading up to his first pitch.

Before his fifth major league start, Hernández told reporters that Castro would likely be watching him pitch against the Mets and added, "He knows everything." With José Cardenal, the Yankees' Cuban-born coach, translating for him, Hernández spoke for about 15 minutes. It was his version of an opening monologue before the show.

After talking and talking, Hernández proceeded to tossing and tossing and held the Mets without a hit into the sixth inning. He threw 142 pitches and allowed one run on two singles in eight innings. And he wanted to keep pitching. Of course, he did.

"In Cuba, you don't have a relief pitcher every time out," Hernández said. "In Cuba, it's win or die."

On that night, Torre almost had to rip the baseball out of Hernández's hand.

"I remember I took the ball from him and he didn't let it go," Torre said. "And he just had this confused look on his face. I came to realize that he had never really been taken out of a game before. But he was a master. He could paint the corners with the best of them."

As masterful as Hernández could be, there were some moments when he was mortal. On July 31, Hernández was battered for 10 runs on 13 hits in five and one-third innings in a 10–5 loss to the Angels. Some pitchers have never had such unsightly statistics in an outing, but Hernández had that ugly performance in his 10th start.

After the debacle, the Yankees counseled Hernández about the importance of pitching inside more because left-handed batters were waiting on his outside pitches and capitalizing on them. The Angels' lefty batters were 9 for 13 in the game as El Duque tried to nick the outside corner with his slider, curve, and changeup. Hernández listened to the advice, admitted he had to adjust, and did. Two weeks later, Hernández struck out 13 and took a shutout into the ninth inning in a 2–0 win over the Rangers. El Duque allowed one hit in 12 at-bats to lefty hitters, which caused a cranky Will Clark to call him "a 40-year-old rookie." Hernández's teammates noticed how he countered.

"Duque, man, what can I say about Duque?" said shortstop Derek Jeter. "We hadn't really seen his type of pitcher. We hadn't seen someone who was like him and who would throw from so many different arm angles in the span of one at-bat. And he would throw any pitch at any time. He was afraid of nothing and no one."

The teammate who could offer the best perspective on Hernández was Posada, who was as headstrong and combative as the pitcher he caught. Of the 23 starts that Hernández made in the regular season and postseason in 1998, Posada caught 21 of them. All these years later, Posada searched for the optimal way to describe El Duque.

"He was just perfection," Posada said. "He was so... Well, perfection is a word, but I'm not sure it's the word I'm looking for. He wasn't nervous. He went through hell and now he's living his childhood dream. He was just saying, 'I'm here. This is the best time of my life and I'm not going to take anything for granted.' Yeah, I guess perfection is the word I wanted to use."

How often does a catcher use the word *perfection* to describe a pitcher? Posada actually caught David Wells's perfect game on May 17, 1998, and he had a strong and close relationship with the left-hander. But, when I interviewed Posada for this book, he never used the word *perfection* to describe Wells. Posada made several complimentary remarks about Wells, but he stopped short of saying "perfection." Yet that was the word that he summoned to describe Hernández.

From 60 feet and 6 inches away, Posada flashed signs to a pitcher who was in control, always in control. When it was Hernández's day to pitch, it was his pace, his pitches, and his decisions. El Duque was fearless, navigating his way through a lineup to get to the situations he preferred. If that meant walking the powerful Jim Thome to load the bases and face the equally imposing Manny Ramírez, a right-handed batter, that's what Hernández would do.

"Talk about balls," Posada said. "This freaking guy had balls. He was unfazed. He would do things that no other pitcher would ever do. But I think that's because of who he was and where he came from and what he had to go through to get here. It was just crazy."

In the emotional and caring Posada, the Yankees had the ideal catcher to handle Hernández. Initially, Hernández wasn't sure who he could trust, but he quickly trusted Posada, and for obvious reasons. Posada respected Hernández and felt an immediate kinship with El Duque because Posada's father had also defected from Cuba 30 years earlier. Before Posada heard one fact about Hernández's harrowing exit from Cuba, the catcher already knew what was in Hernández's heart because that's what had been in his father's heart.

Frustrated and unsettled by Castro's leadership in Cuba,

Jorge Posada Sr. stowed away on a tobacco ship with a bottle of water and a credit card in 1968. When the ship docked in Greece, Posada Sr. jumped off before the cargo was unloaded and disappeared into the woods. He hid there for 24 hours, waiting for his clothes to dry and for the boat to depart. Eventually, Posada Sr. traveled to New York and then to Spain and met his parents in Puerto Rico four months after his journey began.

"In Cuba, I lived with Fidel Castro for eight years," the elder Posada said. "It's crazy, you know? I was surprised I could ever get away."

That's the way El Duque felt too. And when the younger Posada watched how competitive Hernández was, it reminded him of his father's competitiveness. Posada's father implored his son to use wooden bats and insisted that he learn how to bat left-handed so that he could become a switch-hitter. Those experiments weren't easy for an 11-year-old who longed to hear the ping of an aluminum bat and who struck out in 21 straight at-bats as a lefty hitter. But Posada Jr., who was as competitive as his dad or Hernández, persisted. He hit a homer in his 22nd at-bat and waved to his father, who was coaching the opposing team, as he rounded third base.

Yes, Posada was surely the right man to guide El Duque.

"I told him all about my dad and, of course, it brought us closer," Posada said. "He knew that my dad was a prisoner because of communism. We talked about it. He knew all of it."

Hernández leaned heavily on Posada. Because Posada was bilingual and spoke English and Spanish, El Duque communicated with Posada in Spanish. And, if one of El Duque's teammates spoke to him in English, Posada would translate for him.

"He truly helped me," Hernández said. "He was a brother for me then and is a brother for me today."

But brothers fight. They push and punch and they scream and shout. Posada and Hernández were no different than any brothers because, as much as they loved each other, they had some verbal skirmishes. And, on one occasion, the two of them had to be separated by teammates as a verbal tussle turned physical.

"Yeah, we fought," Posada said. "It wasn't in 1998. I think it was in his last year with the Yankees. We had a little fight in the clubhouse. It was just stupid stuff. I don't even remember what it was about. They had to separate us. It's just like your brother. You argue and then, all of a sudden, you're ready to throw punches."

But Posada considered the fight one page in a 400-page friendship.

"I don't remember what it was about and he probably doesn't remember," Posada said. "It doesn't matter. We're still friends."

Hernández agreed with Posada's assessment.

"We have a great relationship, but, to be honest, not everything was a bed of roses," Hernández said. "We had lots of disagreements. We clashed a lot because we were both temperamental. But maybe that helped us. It helped me a lot to focus on the game, to try and be stronger and to execute. Jorge was a very big help to me."

Posada's fervent approach impressed Joe Girardi, the man

who Posada supplanted to garner more playing time at catcher in 1998. Posada played in 111 games while Girardi played in 78. Not only did Posada help Hernández transition to the major leagues, Girardi said Posada brought a passion that impacted the rest of the Yankees.

"Jorgie was tough, really tough," Girardi said. "It was a dog-fight every game for Jorgie. Jorgie's attitude was infectious. And maybe he doesn't get enough credit for the attitude that he brought every day. He came to the park and said, 'We're going to do whatever it takes to win. If we have to do this or that, we're going to do whatever it takes to beat you.' Jorgie had some kind of intensity that he brought to the field every day. It was special."

The special catcher watched over a special pitcher in El Duque. A few years after Hernández's arrival in New York, he was pitching with some shoulder soreness. A teammate inquired about the injury and asked Hernández if he would still be able to pitch through the discomfort. Hernández stared at the concerned Yankee, shook his head with disdain, and said, "I don't pitch with this" and pointed to his shoulder. And then Hernández wrapped his hands around his crotch and said, "I pitch with these."

Crude? Probably. True? Absolutely.

Soon after El Duque cited his Yankees' debut as his favorite memory, he gushed about another game that also ranks atop his list of memories: his win over the Cleveland Indians in Game 4 of the ALCS. That season-saving victory is the performance that is most associated with El Duque because he really did rescue and resuscitate the Yankees' season.

After a tumultuous first week in which the Yankees started

1–4 and both the manager and general manager wondered about their job security, the Yankees had cruised and coasted their way through an idyllic season. Pressure? What pressure? The Yankees kept winning and winning so there was not much stress. Until Game 4. Until they trailed the Indians two games to one in a best of seven series.

"It was really the first time all year that we were worried," said right fielder Paul O'Neill.

Enter El Duque. Enter an unflappable ace, claiming that he treated the pressure-packed game the same as any other game, Hernández pitched seven scoreless innings as the Yankees won, 4–0. With that one win, Hernández allowed the Yankees to exhale. The plans for a World Series parade could be revived. Hernández said he "didn't put pressure" on himself and "focused on the positives" swirling around him. In Chapter 8, I will write much more about Hernández's approach and his antics on that day and what his teammates felt before and after the monumental game.

Throughout Hernández's spellbinding journey, Cashman was thankful that he had displayed some civility to Cubas in 1994 because he thinks it helped the Yankees in 1998. Mariano Rivera was a Double-A pitcher at the time and he had hired Cubas to replace New York–based Irwin Weiner as his agent. But General Manager Gene Michael was friends with Weiner and he told Cashman that Cubas "stole" Rivera.

The Yankees held spring training in Fort Lauderdale and their offices were in white trailers a 30-second walk from the ballpark. After one workout day, Cubas wanted to meet with Michael to discuss Rivera.

"I'm not letting that guy in here," Michael barked. "He stole a player from my friend."

Cashman reminded Michael that players choose their own agents and that the Yankees must honor that process and communicate with the representatives.

"Well, if you want to meet with him, you can meet with him," Michael said. "But do it outside these trailers. I'm not letting him in here."

Needing to appease his boss and also needing to keep Cubas from knowing Michael's unfriendly position, Cashman left the trailer and suggested to Cubas that they chat outside. Cubas agreed. The Yankees' workout was over for the day so the two men sat in the empty ballpark and had an hour-long conversation about Rivera and his next contract. They made progress and shook hands. And Cubas never knew that Michael, who was known as Stick, wanted him banished from the Yankees' offices.

"I didn't agree with Stick on this," Cashman said. "I just treated Cubas like a human being."

That behavior proved fortuitous.

"A few years later, it's '98 and Joe Cubas now has the most famous Cuban baseball player out there," Cashman said. "And he said, 'I know one thing, the only guy I want to deal with is Brian Cashman because, when I was a nobody, he was the only person who showed me respect.'"

For Cashman, there was a life lesson, not just a baseball lesson, in the way he acted.

"So I always tell people, along the way, to treat people the way they deserve to be treated, whether you think they can do something for you or not," Cashman said. "You have no idea whether someone might be able to help you later in life. And that's not the reason to do it. You should treat people nicely anyway. But that paid dividends for us. It wasn't just that we wrote the check for El Duque. It helped that I already had a good relationship with Joe Cubas."

Still, even though Cashman had a relationship with Cubas, he was hesitant about pursuing Hernández because of the Irabu experience, the Yankees' last major international addition. The Yankees had acquired Irabu and Homer Bush from the San Diego Padres for three players and $3 million in 1997. Irabu had refused to sign with the Padres and said he only wanted to play for the Yankees. But, after Irabu pitched strongly in a 10–3 win over the Detroit Tigers in front of 51,901 fans at Yankee Stadium in his debut, he sputtered. He allowed five earned runs or more in six of his next eight appearances and seemed uncomfortable. He's the only player I've ever covered who glared at reporters and then drew an imaginary perimeter around his locker to tell them to stay away.

Anyway, as Cashman expressed reservations about pursuing Hernández because of Irabu's shoddy start, Gordon Blakeley, the Yankees' director of player personnel, delivered a pointed message.

"Cash," Blakeley said, "if you get gun-shy because something in the past didn't work out, you might miss out on the next MVP or Cy Young Award winner."

Those words resonated with Cashman.

"You've got to trust your scouts, trust your people, and trust your process," Cashman said. "And, if you have enough people who are collectively willing to bet on this and you have the flexibility to do it, then you do it. So we went all in."

And it was the right decision. It was the perfect decision.

El Duque was a physical specimen, a sinewy and athletic pitcher who wanted to throw and throw and throw. One day, I was having a conversation with Cone about the physicality of being a pitcher and the strength and durability it takes to throw 100 or more pitches and do it again five days later. Cone, who was five-foot-eleven and 185 pounds, explained how a pitcher's power comes "from the ground up" and that's why it was important to have powerful legs. Despite his smallish size, Cone had thick legs and used them to push off the rubber and extend closer to the plate before releasing the ball. A flexible upper body was vital too.

When I asked Cone to describe the perfect pitcher's body, he laughed and said, "I will take El Duque's body." Cone laughed, but he meant it. He would have selected El Duque as his stunt pitcher.

"A perfect pitcher would have extreme strength in the lower half of his body," Cone said. "The foundation is to have very strong legs, but to still have a very flexible upper body. They're almost completely opposed to each other. Generally, if you have a strong lower half, you'd have a big, symmetrical upper half. But that's not the case with pitchers. You'd want someone with a nice, long wingspan and extreme flexibility in the upper half."

Do you want to guess who had those things? El Duque. He looked like he had been molded out of granite and had "the strongest legs" of any pitcher Cone had ever seen.

"El Duque wasn't overly bulky in his chest, but his legs were rock solid," Cone said. "That's how he did that leg kick all of those years. He had the legs of Mikhail Baryshnikov. He was strong, muscular, and stout in the lower half. And he had the upper body of Roger Federer. He was lanky and flexible. You want to have strength in your upper body, but you want the ability to get maximum extension in the upper half with your throwing arm. The combination of both allows you to get better extension with the length of your stride and to get your release point out in front of you to cut down on the distance to the plate. And El Duque had all of that going for him."

If El Duque had a biggest fan in the Yankees' clubhouse, it was Cone. As one of the most creative pitchers in the majors, Cone was enamored with Hernández because Hernández was probably even more creative. He had so many arm angles, whether he threw sidearm or three-quarters or over the top. He threw so many pitches at so many different speeds, teasing and tempting hitters. And he was so stubborn, in a good way. When Cone watched Hernández float first-pitch curves for quick strikes to left-handed batters, he said to himself, "Why didn't I think of that?"

"A slow, looping curve from a righty to a left-handed batter is a great way to steal a strike," Cone said. "It's like a softball pitch. It's not a pitch they want to swing at. They're trying to get a good pitch to hit, preferably a fastball. El Duque taught me the value of that first-pitch curve."

But their relationship was an equal opportunity relationship because Cone also gave El Duque some lessons. When Cone watched Hernández warming up before a game in Oakland, he noticed that Hernández wasn't being aggressive with his changeup, a relatively new pitch. Cone explained to El Duque that he should throw the pitch with the same power as a fastball to get the most spin on the ball.

While Hernández seemed receptive to Cone's advice, he misplaced a few changes in a subsequent game and stopped throwing the pitch. Cone was disappointed so he marched up to Hernández and said, "Finito. Cambio. Finito." Although Cone combined two languages, El Duque understood. "Finish the changeup." Throw the change the same way you throw a fastball, Cone said. Hernández obeyed, he threw some nifty changes and gave Cone a high five in the dugout.

How impactful was that advice from Cone? When Hernández faced the Indians in the ALCS, he unveiled the change, a pitch they really weren't expecting. In fact, with a 3–0 lead and runners on base in the sixth inning, Hernández whiffed Thome on a 3–2 change. It was a fearless choice. It was typical El Duque.

For the mighty Yankees to add Hernández to an already strong pitching staff seemed unfair. Before Hernández's arrival, the Yankees had a rotation that featured David Wells, Cone, Andy Pettitte, Irabu, and Mendoza. Wells had pitched a perfect game in May and would have the best season of his career. After recovering quickly enough from shoulder surgery to make the Opening Day roster, Cone was blitzed in his first two starts. Cone also learned that a tumor was discovered on his mother's lung. He toyed with the idea of retiring, but Cone didn't and won 15 games and had a 2.71 ERA in his last 23 starts. Pettitte had an inconsistent season, for him, but he still won 16 games, pitched 216⅓ innings, and won the World Series clincher. While Wells had the perfect game in May, Irabu was actually the American League's Pitcher of the Month as he went 4–1 with a 1.44 E.R.A. The beleaguered Irabu still led the league with a 2.47 ERA in late June before fading. The underrated Mendoza won 10 games, pitched 130⅓ innings, and never complained about his evolving role.

"The 1998 team had the perfect balance in the rotation," Cone said. "You had two strong left-handed pitchers in Wells and Pettitte who threw to both sides of the plate and were tough on lefties. And you had me and El Duque and we were tough on righties. We could exploit mediocre right-handed hitters with sliders and different arm angles. Stylistically, the hitters got different looks every game."

That balance is why Cone questioned the trade that sent Wells and two others to the Blue Jays for Roger Clemens in the spring of 1999.

"As great as Rocket was, I thought we lost some balance when we lost a lefty like Wells," Cone said. "But we won the World Series the next two years so it's hard to argue with. I just thought the balance of the '98 rotation gave us a different dynamic."

Meanwhile, the bullpen dynamic centered around Mariano Rivera, of course. After Rivera strained his right groin in April, he missed 18 days. Still, Rivera was calm and patient as he watched a talented team perform without him. And, once

Rivera returned, that team became even more dominant and more intimidating at the end of games. He was 3–0 with a 1.91 ERA and 36 saves in 41 chances that season. Interestingly, Rivera, who averaged over eight strikeouts per nine innings in his career, averaged a career low of 5.3 per nine innings that season. He induced lots of contact, weak contact.

I have never covered a more peaceful and more confident player than Rivera. Before games, Rivera could usually be found reading a book, often the Bible, by his locker. He was welcoming to all. I never felt as if I was interviewing Rivera. I always felt as if we were having a conversation because he would answer questions and he would also ask questions. During one conversation in 1996, Rivera happily told me how he made a baseball glove out of cardboard when he was a seven-year-old growing up in Panama. And then Rivera reached into his locker, grabbed the lid of a shoebox and explained how that cardboard could be transformed into a glove. Rivera didn't own his first real baseball glove until he was 10 years old.

As much as Rivera's 1997 is remembered for the homer he allowed to Sandy Alomar Jr. in the postseason, it should also be remembered as the season when he discovered his one of a kind cut fastball. On a random June afternoon, Rivera and Mendoza were playing catch along the outfield grass before a game, as they always did. But, on this day, something phenomenal happened.

With every four-seam fastball Rivera threw, the baseball darted so much that Mendoza became annoyed and told Rivera to stop playing around with him. But Rivera insisted he wasn't doing anything different and that the late and cutting movement on the pitch came naturally. At first, Rivera tried to eliminate the cutting action on the pitch to just throw a four-seam fastball, but he and the Yankees realized that was senseless. Rivera had stumbled upon an amazing weapon and he needed to use the cutter, as is.

"It was," Rivera said, "a gift from God."

From a casual game of catch, Rivera wound up with a pitch that helped carry the Yankees to perennial glory and also helped carry him to the Hall of Fame. Since Rivera threw the pitch with a four-seam grip, he never lost velocity on his cutter and still had the late-breaking right-to-left cutting action. Most pitchers lose velocity on their cutters, but Rivera maintained that peak velocity and that's why he shattered so many bats and produced so many feeble swings. The pitch zoomed in on left-handed batters and tied them up and that pitch helped make Rivera the greatest closer of all time.

Baseball players are often tense or intense, but teammates marveled at how relaxed Rivera was, with Cone saying Mariano looked like he "was barely breathing." Rivera was a slave to his routine, which included hanging out in the clubhouse for the first three or four innings, getting a massage, and then hopping in a golf cart and riding through the bowels of the stadium to get to the bullpen. Usually, an expeditious three-out save was forthcoming.

"He was very confident, but calm," Cone said. "It was like he didn't even have a pulse."

Before Joe Torre gave the baseball to a confident Rivera, he often used left-hander Mike Stanton as one of his primary set-up men. Stanton was cool and confident, a pitcher who attacked hitters in the aggressive way he used to attack receivers as a high school defensive back. Some antsy relievers seem like they're ready to chew off their fingernails in the bullpen. Not Stanton. He had pitched for the Atlanta Braves in the 1991 World Series and 1998 was the seventh time he had pitched in the postseason. He liked and embraced the pressure.

"Joe Torre used to tell us, 'If you can't pitch today, don't put your spikes on because, if you put them on, I might use you because we have a game to win today,'" Stanton recalled. "And he said we'd worry about tomorrow tomorrow. I think that kind of attitude and that kind of tenacity was there for the whole team."

Teammates raved about Stanton's contributions that season so it's surprising that he had a 5.47 ERA. Stanton said he was "notorious for having that one bad third of an inning" and he was telling the truth. Stanton allowed 48 earned runs in 79 innings across 67 games. But Stanton allowed 24 of those runs in THREE INNINGS across six appearances. While a pitcher's statistics are his statistics, Stanton's ERA in the 61 other games in which he wasn't destroyed was a tidy 2.86.

If Torre needed a reliever to retire a right-handed batter, he typically called Jeff Nelson. At six-foot-eight, Nelson was tall and tough. But, more importantly, he had a vicious slider that befuddled hitters, sweeping across the plate like a Frisbee. Still, it was an exasperating season for Nelson because he injured his back during the May brawl with the Orioles. After Armando Benítez intentionally drilled Tino Martinez, Nelson was involved in the pursuit of Benítez and even tossed a few wayward punches. He missed more than two months that season and the Yankees spoke ominously in July and August about whether Nelson would return at all. Nelson complained about "pain shooting down" his legs and it was discovered that he had an inflamed lower back caused by a bulging disc.

When a player was injured, the Yankees usually shipped him to their spring training facility in Tampa to rehabilitate. It was a policy Steinbrenner preferred. As Nelson explained Steinbrenner's logic, he said, "I think he thought you might heal a little bit quicker if you had to get up at 7 a.m. every morning and head to the field. And it was true. When you were down there, you were thinking, 'OK, I have to do anything I can to heal and get out of here.'"

Beyond the 7 a.m. wake-up calls, Steinbrenner was instrumental in Nelson recuperating and eventually returning to the Yankees. Steinbrenner recommended a chiropractor to Nelson and the pitcher went twice a day for three straight days and, after those adjustments, Nelson's pain subsided. "I wish I had seen him a lot sooner because it was the only thing that worked," he said. Nelson came back to New York with a vengeance and allowed no runs and one hit in nine September appearances. Since Nelson had held right-handed batters to a .202 average and had whiffed them a third of the time in 1996 and 1997, he was an important weapon for the postseason.

Nelson wasn't the only six-foot-eight reliever in the bullpen. Graeme Lloyd, a mild-mannered and likable Australian, was also six-foot-eight and he was a lefty specialist. And he was adept at it. Lloyd pitched in 50 games, faced only 145 batters, and held them to a .191 average and a .294 slugging percentage.

But Lloyd's Yankee career didn't start too smoothly. After the Yankees acquired him from the Milwaukee Brewers in August 1996, he was pounded for 11 earned runs in five and two-thirds innings and was vilified. But Lloyd stayed quiet, stayed confident, and rebounded with eight scoreless appearances in the postseason. He found a home in the Bronx.

Mike Buddie, the rookie reliever, described how Lloyd was the first pitcher or coach to lecture him about the difference in the slope between the bullpen mound and the game mound. After warming up to go into a game, Lloyd told Buddie he needed to know "where your front foot needs to be when your arm is at its release point" because that eliminates the slope of the mound from the equation.

"I thought Graeme was this goofy guy, but he really understood how to execute his pitches," Buddie said. "I had never had that kind of analytical thought process."

When I reached Lloyd by phone in Australia and explained the premise of my book and how I had already interviewed Jeter, Posada, Pettitte, Cone, O'Neill, and others, he playfully said, "You've already got all of them. Why do you need me?"

But the Yankees needed Lloyd, Nelson, Stanton, Mendoza, and Darren Holmes to help build a bridge to Rivera at the end of games. When the Yankees had a lead after seven innings, they were 93–1.

"Our bullpen was so good," said center fielder Bernie Williams. "They locked games down. When we had a lead after the seventh inning, the game was over."

Still, on a staff that included a perfect game pitcher in Wells, a two-time 20-game winner and a perfect game pitcher-in-waiting in Cone, a future Hall of Famer in Rivera, and a postseason stalwart in Pettitte, the most fascinating pitcher was the one who showed up in the majors in June and did everything so deftly and so differently.

In addition to Hernández's season-saving ALCS win over the Indians, he made one other postseason start in Game 2 of the World Series. The Yankees bolted to a 6–0 lead in the first two innings and Hernández did the rest in silencing the Padres across seven innings. Afterward, Tony Gwynn, the hitting technician, praised Hernández for getting ahead in counts, changing speeds with all of his pitches, and even switching sides of the rubber to help with angles on pitches to further confuse the batters.

"He didn't look rattled," Gwynn said.

But, even as Hernández smiled through an incredible season with the Yankees, he was incredibly lonely because his family was still in Cuba. On numerous occasions, Hernández would weep and would confide in Cardenal about how much he missed his daughters, who were eight years old and three years old, and his mother. Hernández spoke with them, but he hadn't seen his family since he left Cuba and he didn't know when or if he would see them. El Duque's abundant joy was shrouded in sadness.

Behind the scenes, the energetic Cubas worked for more than a month to try and get Hernández's family permission to leave Cuba and visit him in New York. With the hatred and the animosity that existed between Castro and Hernández, there was considerable doubt about whether Castro would actually extend the favor. After John Cardinal

O'Connor, the archbishop of New York, intervened and sent an emissary to Castro to make that request for Hernández, Castro acquiesced.

That development was shocking. Castro had called El Duque a "mercenary" who had "betrayed his country" and Hernández wasn't shy about tweaking Castro once he signed with the Yankees. Still, Hernández's two daughters, Yahumara and Steffi, his mother, Maria Julia Pedrosa-Cruz, and his former wife, Norma Elvira Manso, were granted 30-day visas. The deliriously happy family arrived in time to attend the Yankees' championship parade along Broadway. Ten months of anxiety culminated in an explosion of tears when Hernández was finally reunited with his loved ones.

"Right after we won the World Series, they had a plane bringing his family from Cuba to New York," Posada said. "Can you imagine that? It's 25 years later and I get goose bumps just thinking about it. It's just unbelievable."

Unbelievable, but very believable. The mystery man's story kept getting sweeter and more poignant.

CHAPTER 5

The Joy of Jeter

Life was good for Derek Jeter. Life always seemed to be good for Derek Jeter. He was the 23-year-old shortstop for the New York Yankees and he was one of the most popular and respected players in the major leagues. He had one World Series ring on his finger from his memorable rookie season in 1996 and he was searching for more with a very powerful team in 1998. Yes, life was definitely good.

Since Jeter had told his parents as a young boy that his dream was to play shortstop for the Yankees, the same out-of-this-world dream shared by millions, he really was living the dream. Who is that prescient? How does a kid from Kalamazoo, Michigan, with a Yankees uniform hanging on his bedroom wall dream the biggest of dreams into existence? And how does he feel when that dream is realized?

"When you're a kid and you're dreaming of playing in the major leagues, you just envision yourself there," Jeter said. "Nothing else comes along with it. It's almost like it's a black-and-white picture. And, once you're there, you start to put color on the picture. And, with my dream, it's like I've never woken up."

But, before the Yankees played their first game of 1998, Jeter wondered if he would even get to play that season. For a brief and horrifying minute or so, he wrestled with his own mortality.

After the Yankees completed their spring training schedule in Tampa, they were a confident and restless bunch, ready to start a new season and erase the ignominy of what happened in 1997. The day that players leave their spring training site to begin a new year is always filled with anticipation, excitement, and relief because the 45 days of practicing and playing exhibition games has finally ended. The real season has arrived.

But, before starting the real season, the Yankees were traveling to San Diego to play an exhibition game against San Diego State. It sounded like a simple pit stop for to play against some giddy college players before starting the season in Anaheim against the Angels. As Jeter recalled, it ended up being far from simple. It ended up being terrifying.

Since the Yankees were flying in an internationally based aircraft that had already landed in Tampa, the plane wasn't permitted to make a second consecutive stop in the United States. That meant the Yankees couldn't simply fly directly from Tampa to San Diego. Instead, the decision was made to have the 747 fly from Tampa to Tijuana, Mexico, and then transport the team to San Diego by bus. It seemed like a minor travel adjustment, until it wasn't.

When Jeter and his teammates landed in Tijuana and

climbed on the bus, they could see the United States–Mexico border ahead of them. So far, so good. The driver soon turned the trip into chaos and distress when he made a reckless turn and began driving atop the two-foot cement barriers that lined the exit to the airport. The Yankees were jostled inside the bus as two wheels were rumbling on top of the barrier and two wheels were still slicing along the road. For a few frightening moments, which felt like a lot more than a few moments, the bus felt as if it were going to topple over and crash.

"We were on our bus and the bus ran into the median and it almost flipped," Jeter said. "We were sort of teetering. I just remember people yelling to get to the other side of the bus and to try and tip it back so it wouldn't flip over. We hadn't even played one game yet. So our season almost started horrifically."

Reliever Mike Stanton recalled how the driver was trying to regale the players with information about the area over the loudspeaker. He droned on too long, Stanton said. Perhaps he became distracted.

"I was sitting right behind the bus driver and the bus driver decided that he was going to give a tour," Stanton said. "So he is on the mic and he's talking and we get up to the border and it was kind of dark and there weren't any streetlights. And he's still talking. And, I mean, the guys in the back are just killing him. They are trying to get him to stop. And he just kept going and going. At one point, one of us just said, 'Dude, please, just stop talking. Please, just drive the bus.'"

That request wasn't exactly followed. While the driver did drive the bus, he collided with the barriers. Jeter doesn't remember who was sitting beside him, but David Cone recalled how a panicky Hideki Irabu was next to him and Jeff Nelson was bracing for David Wells to come crashing across the aisle. Stanton remembered a lot of screaming and a lot of howling. The bus kept teetering and kept riding on two wheels, which put the wherewithal of the $63 million Yankees in jeopardy. Million-dollar arms and legs and bodies aren't supposed to get smashed around like pinballs.

Eventually, just as it seemed the bus might crash on its side, the driver managed to regain control and steady the vehicle so that he was driving on four wheels. Every passenger bounced around as the bus stabilized with a bang. But it was back on four wheels. Once the players realized they were safe, they exhaled and then screamed at the reckless driver. He was so shaken up that he stopped driving and parked the bus in the middle of the road. The angry and relieved players jumped off the bus and walked the short distance to the border.

"That incident," said Jeter, "is the thing I remember the most from the beginning of the 1998 season."

The crazy bus ride. The crazy and almost disastrous bus ride. When I asked Jeter to recount something unbelievable that happened in 1998, he chose the bus ride. That was more unbelievable than the 1–4 start, more unbelievable than Joe Torre's motivational clubhouse meeting in Seattle, and more unbelievable than speculation about Torre's job status. That's how harrowing that bus ride was.

Searching for the most precise details, I asked Jeter which side of the bus almost tipped over. Stanton had said the driver was shifting from the right lane to the left lane so the bus almost fell over on its left side. How did Jeter remember it tipping? To the left or the right? Jeter laughed.

"I don't know which side," Jeter said, "I'm tipping to right now."

But, typically, Jeter knew exactly where he was and who he was in 1998. He almost always did. That was the beauty and strength of Jeter, who was a calm and confident player from the first day he donned pinstripes. Cone recalled how Jeter always seemed to say and do the right thing, even as a 21-year-old. The Yankees had mostly moved beyond the notion of hazing young players when Jeter became the full-time shortstop in 1996, Cone said. But, even if that immature ritual had still existed, Cone said there wasn't anything to roast Jeter about as a rookie.

As a veteran, Cone was always eyeballing young players to try and gauge how they would fit in. Some of the questions Cone had were: How does he prepare? How does he interact with his teammates? How much does he talk about himself and not the team? Can he be trusted? How passionate is he? How badly does he want to win?

Every time Cone asked himself those questions about Jeter, the answers came easily and came quickly. Jeter was prepared, passionate, and respectful and wanted to win as desperately as anyone in the Yankees' clubhouse. Within months of becoming the starter, Jeter had also become a leader. And Cone was thrilled with that because the Yankees needed a dependable shortstop. They got more, in fact. They got a rock star who also happened to play shortstop at an elite level.

"Derek has a very even-keeled personality and that was

something that helped our team and helped calm our team," Cone said. "In so many ways, Derek was made to play in New York. He was a great player who became even better when the stakes were higher. That's not easy to do, especially in New York."

As the Yankees were watching Jeter, he was watching them too. Well, to be more specific, he knew they were watching him.

"I always just tried to be accountable," Jeter said. "I think players look at their teammates and ask: Are they going to be responsible? Are they going to speak to the media when things go bad or are they going to run out of the clubhouse? Maybe my teammates saw that I was more inclined to run out of the clubhouse when I had a good game as opposed to when I struggled. And I think that stands out for the veteran guys. If you're a veteran guy and you're stuck there answering questions about a teammate, it tends to irritate you a little bit."

By the time 1998 arrived, Jeter wasn't trying to prove himself anymore. He was one of the leaders on a team packed with veterans. Even in a harmonious clubhouse filled with savvy players like Cone, Paul O'Neill, Tino Martinez, Darryl Strawberry, Joe Girardi, Tim Raines, and Chili Davis, Jeter found a way to be a leader. He was a quiet leader, but he was also an impactful leader. Just by the way he played and just by the way he acted.

Jeter was addicted to his routine and his routine was a year-round dedication to baseball. About two weeks after the Yankees had that depressing loss to the Indians in 1997, Jeter was already working out at the team's complex in Tampa, Florida. That had become Jeter's routine: grind through a full season in which he expected to play every day, try to excel in the post-season, take about two weeks off as a vacation, and return to baseball activities sometime in November. With or without a new World Series ring, that's how Jeter behaved.

"It was just a desire to keep improving," Jeter said. "I moved to Tampa to be close to our facilities and our coaches and to make myself a better player."

Jeter was beginning his third full season in 1998, but teammates had already noticed his confidence, his devotion, and his desire to win. As unassuming as Jeter was when he spoke with fans from the on-deck circles or as polite as he was when he chatted with a player on second base, teammates said he was an assassin in the way he wanted to win. Jeter didn't need to scream at his teammates. His play screamed for him.

"Looking around the clubhouse in 1998 brought confidence," said reliever Jeff Nelson. "But, it's funny, and you don't want to pinpoint one player, but it was Jeter who really helped bring that winning mentality. It was the way he went out on the field and the way he carried himself. It impacted you as a teammate. I know it impacted me."

In what way?

"Everybody followed his lead," Nelson said. "He had such a passion to win. It wasn't like we thought, 'Oh, we're going to let him down if we don't give it everything we got.' But everybody seemed to follow the guy. I know he was named the captain several years later (in 2003). But he was the captain then and it was only his third year in the big leagues."

Jorge Posada, who was Jeter's best friend on the team, said, "Jeter was one of the leaders, but he didn't even say much then. He just went out there and played every day. That's all he needed to do. That's showing leadership without even having to say anything, but just doing it. Sometimes, that's the best thing a player could do."

At the old Yankee Stadium, the players would exit the clubhouse through a heavy black door, walk a few steps, and descend a turf-covered ramp that took them into the first base dugout. As they moved down the ramp, a blue sign with white lettering was hanging from the ceiling. On that sign was Joe DiMaggio's famous quote: "I want to thank the Good Lord for making me a Yankee." Every time Jeter left the clubhouse and went to play a game in pinstripes, he tapped that sign. Whether it was superstitious or habitual, Jeter felt the need to do it every time.

But it was Jeter's behavior after games in 1998 that impacted one teammate. Darren Holmes, a reliever, was in his first season with the Yankees. After the Yankees won games, Holmes noticed that Jeter would shake hands with his teammates and then announce a random number. "One hundred and fifty-three more," Jeter would say. A week or so later, Holmes heard Jeter bark, "One hundred and forty-eight games to go." Jeter's number was decreasing, but it didn't coincide with the number of games remaining in the regular season. Holmes was confused and asked Paul O'Neill for some clarification.

"That's how many games we've got left until we win the World Series," O'Neill told Holmes.

And Holmes was floored.

"That gave me a completely different view of what was going on there and what we were chasing," Holmes said. "It was like another world was opened up to me. What Derek did actually turned around my whole mindset of what it meant to be a Yankee."

That feeling permeated the clubhouse because Jeter noticed something about the players surrounding him in 1998: Winning wasn't enough. Winning in emphatic fashion was the goal. Before the Yankees dashed onto the field for a game, Jeter said the players didn't have any long discussions or inspirational chats about what they needed to do. Baseball is a sport in which the teams play every day. It's not football, a sport where there is one game a week and the intensity builds all week to that day. In baseball, the approach can't be as intense every day. But, still, even if the players simply nodded and said "Let's go" to each other before taking the field, Jeter said the reminders of the goal ahead were always there: Win every day. Dominate every day.

"I think it was something that was understood," Jeter said. "I don't remember having a lot of conversations about it with guys. But we wanted to not only beat you every day. We wanted to beat you EVERY INNING. You know what I mean? It's tough to say we never took a day off, but, collectively, there weren't many days that we took off. It was a situation where we had guys coming off the bench who felt like they should be starting. So, when you have guys coming off the bench and putting up numbers, that meant they were competing. Every single day, that's what we did. It wasn't something we had to talk about. It was understood."

The wins kept piling up for the Yankees. Famously unaware of statistics, Jeter didn't remember that he started the season with six hits in 35 at-bats and he didn't remember that he had four hits on May 6 to boost his average to .304. And, after that four-hit game, he never hit below .300 for the rest of the season. Jeter, who played with a focused ferocity, just remembered a lot of wins. I told Jeter I called the 1998 Yankees "gentlemanly bullies" because they destroyed teams, but they did it respectfully. He appreciated that nickname and called it an apt description.

"The thing is, we wanted to pummel teams," Jeter said. "We wanted to beat them every single day. It didn't make a difference who we were playing. I thought we were respectful. I didn't think we had any jerks on the team. Or should I say we didn't have a lot of jerks on the team."

Then Jeter chuckled and continued saying, "I thought we were respectful, but we wanted to beat you and that's the only thing that mattered. And, I keep saying it, but that's every single day. We were 125–50, counting the postseason. And, man, to have a regular season like that and then you have to follow it up with the postseason. You have to do it like that when you're the favorites and everyone is gunning for you."

As much as Jeter was a quiet leader, he was also the sort of player who didn't scold teammates off the field. It wasn't his style. So there was no way Jeter would do something like that on the field. Except for the one time that he did.

The Yankees had already won 106 games and were being compared to the best teams of all time when they played the Baltimore Orioles at Camden Yards on September 18. During that game, a pop fly was hit over Jeter's head and into shallow left field. Jeter, left fielder Ricky Ledée, and center fielder Chad Curtis all converged on the ball and none of them caught it. When Wells saw the ball fall to the grass, he spread his arms wide and expressed his dissatisfaction. It isn't the kind of move that ingratiates one teammate to another and Jeter moved swiftly to let Wells know that. When Jeter returned the baseball to Wells, he said sharply, "We don't do that shit around here."

Jeter explained that he was simply and emphatically reminding Wells that the Yankees were near the end of a phenomenal season and that they needed to focus on baseball. Nothing else.

"That was it," Jeter said. "That's what I was doing. You know David Wells. I mean, I have no issues with Boomer. I've never had any issues with Boomer. He's animated. I get it. He's animated and he threw his arms up in the air. I just said, 'We don't do that shit around here.'"

The chatty Wells was an animated sort and he was clearly animated after that miscue.

"It was a catchable ball and it was up there and I was like, 'Are you kidding me?'" Wells said. "When a ball is hanging that long, somebody has got to get it and nobody took control. And I just threw my hands up. It was just a reaction. It wasn't against anybody. That's one thing I never did was show my teammates up. I knew better than that."

Still, Jeter thought Wells's actions were unnecessary and immediately let the pitcher know how he felt.

"I respected Derek for doing that because nobody wants to

be shown up on the field," Wells said. "But I didn't feel that I showed him up. I remember Derek saying, 'We don't do that shit around here.' I didn't like it, but I respected it. I don't recall if I said anything back to him. If I did, I probably just said, 'Go do your job at shortstop.'"

Despite Wells's frustration over the ball dropping in between three teammates, he actually apologized to Jeter, Ledée, and Curtis. While Wells's actions were seen by many, Buster Olney of the *New York Times* later heard whispers of a possible fight between Wells and Jeter. But, when the reporter tried to pursue the story, Jeter vehemently denied there had been an altercation and rounded up teammates to support his story.

"So the whole thing that I challenged him to a fight?" Jeter said. "That's not true."

As detailed in *The Captain*, the seven-part documentary about Jeter's career, Jeter was aggressive in making sure the back-and-forth between Wells and him didn't grow into anything more than the brief exchange. Jeter sent his message to Wells and now it was back to baseball. Fight? There was never a fight and Jeter didn't want that word printed in the *New York Times* or anywhere else.

"Their job was to get a headline and I wasn't gonna give it to them," Jeter said, in the documentary. "My job was to make sure our team was prepared and our team was ready, and the only thing that mattered to us was winning. I looked at it as a distraction."

With a neck as thick as a telephone pole, a square jaw, and a 230-pound frame, Jason Varitek looked the way a durable major league catcher should look. He was a rookie with the Red Sox in 1998, became a central figure in the intense rivalry with the Yankees, and also became a lifetime hero in Boston when he smashed his glove in Álex Rodríguez's face during a skirmish in 2004. Shortly after that Varitek-Rodríguez tussle, I wasn't surprised to find a Fenway staff member using a picture of Varitek's glove connecting with A-Rod's face as a laptop screen saver.

As influential a personality as Varitek would become, he said he was much quieter in the Red Sox's pregame meetings during his rookie season. He did more listening than talking. Still, unprompted, Varitek explained which player the Red Sox always felt they needed to throttle. That player was Jeter, which clashed with what A-Rod once said. He famously dissed Jeter by telling *Esquire* magazine in 2001, teams never say, "'Don't let Derek beat you.' That's never your concern." Well, that player was Varitek's concern.

"Jeter was tough, man," Varitek said. "He was probably the toughest hitter in their lineup in all those years. There wasn't much margin for error because he covered so much of the plate."

Standing close and leaning out over the plate as he swung, Jeter was almost daring pitchers to throw pitches down the middle or on the outside corner, places he exploited by hitting the ball the opposite way with his inside-out swing. If a pitcher had the ability to throw a sinker under Jeter's hands, that was the spot Varitek tried to exploit.

"I wouldn't say he had a hole," Varitek said. "But, if you had a pitcher with some sinker tilt, it was hard for Jeter to stay inside with a ball that was down and in on him. But not every pitcher has that pitch. Jeter pretty much had 90 percent of the rest of the plate covered. That's a really special player."

As Varitek sat in the third base dugout at Yankee Stadium in September 2022, Aaron Judge, Giancarlo Stanton, and the other Yankees were taking batting practice. It was a warm and sunny day and the sound of the bat against the ball was interspersed with Varitek's words. While Varitek, now a Red Sox coach, was charged with trying to get the 2022 Yankees out on this day, I asked him for scouting reports on those tenacious 1998 Yankees.

We started with Knoblauch, the leadoff hitter. Varitek called Knoblauch a "grinding" player and also considered him annoying, in a complimentary way.

"He was a gnat of an at-bat," Varitek said. "He was just a gnat. He forced you to make pitches over and over. And then he'd take his base hits and move on."

Varitek had already given his evaluation on Jeter so I moved on to Paul O'Neill, who usually hit third for the Yankees.

"He made you work too," Varitek said. "Like a lot of the guys in that lineup, he forced you to pitch to him. You had certain matchups and they stayed true to who they were over and over and over. And they made it tough. You had to make Paul O'Neill very aware of the ball that was in on him. After you did that, you tried to use both sides of the plate. He forced you to be able to throw strikes inside. You just played keep away with some of those guys. And there were different strike zones then too. They were a lot bigger and wider and you could get away with more. They were very good at forcing you to make pitches over and over. They stayed true to who they were. They covered a lot of stuff out over the plate."

How about the switch-hitting Bernie Williams?

"He was very similar to O'Neill," Varitek said. "He would kind of wait things out. You'd throw a pitch, you'd miss your spot and make a mistake and, the next thing you know, he drives in a run."

Then, realizing that he was repeating himself, Varitek said, "You could almost describe all of their hitters in that way, with Jeter being the most special one. With the game on the line and when you needed to make a pitch, Jeter is the guy who could provide the punch."

And the confident Jeter always believed he could and would provide the punch. Jeter's confidence was exemplified in 1999 when Pedro Martínez struck out 17 Yankees and threw a one-hitter. It was one of the most electrifying performances I've ever seen. It was the kind of night where hitters watched how sensational Martínez had been and were thankful and relieved they didn't have to face him again for a while. But not Jeter. Do you know what Jeter recalled about that game? Jeter lamented that he was in on the on-deck circle when the game ended because he wanted another chance against the seemingly unhittable Martínez. That is confidence.

Varitek, who was flashing fingers for Pedro on that night, went back to finishing his 1998 scouting report. The next batter Varitek evaluated was Tino Martinez, who led the team with 28 homers.

"I'm partial to Tino because, when I was a kid who had just signed with Seattle, he was wonderful to me," Varitek said. "As a hitter, I hate grouping them all together, but he made you make pitches. He forced you to command the baseball. Literally, that's the way they were. One through nine, that's who they were."

Even as Varitek repeated some of his remarks about different hitters, we kept talking. I asked him about Jorge Posada, who shared the catching duties with Girardi.

"Jorge was more of an offensive threat than Girardi, even as a young pup back then," Varitek said. "He always came up with the big hit. He was the kind of guy who wanted to play every day. I know Joe played a lot too. But Jorge was a special player to do what he did in his career while playing that position."

I had to get Varitek's take on Shane Spencer, the power hitter whom the Yankees called "The Natural" because of the way he exploded onto the scene. Spencer forced his way into the lineup in September and had 10 homers in 67 at-bats, including three grand slams, that season.

"Sometimes, the newness of it helps and the timing of it helps and someone who is new to the league is able to capitalize on mistakes right away," Varitek said. "If I remember it right, he did it with damage when he came up. That's an example of how it takes a whole organization to win a championship. It doesn't just take 25 guys. It takes your whole roster. The unexpected guys, like a Brosius and a Spencer, that's what gets you over the hump."

Oh, yes, Scott Brosius. We saved one of the best hitters for last. Even though Brosius hit eighth or ninth in 135 of the 148 games he started (147 at third base and one at first base), he was one of the Yankees' most productive hitters and made pitchers work and work some more.

"You had your staples in that lineup, but what stands out very much to me from that season was Brosius," Varitek said. "He seemed to come up with big hit after big hit that year."

The return to respectability and relevancy for the Yankees started when they hired Buck Showalter as the manager in 1992 and he teamed with General Manager Gene "Stick" Michael to revamp the club. At the time, George Steinbrenner was serving a lifetime banishment from baseball for paying Howard Spira, a known gambler, $40,000 to uncover incriminating information on Dave Winfield. The ban was later reduced to 30 months. Michael and Showalter targeted talented players with strong work habits while also trying to eliminate any problematic personalities. So the Yankees signed or acquired the likes of Jimmy Key, Paul O'Neill, Wade Boggs, Dion James, Mike Gallego, and Mike Stanley.

In conjunction with that infusion of players, Michael was also keen on having a lineup filled with players who could get on base. Before games, Michael would study a Yankees' statistical sheet and circle how many hits AND how many walks a player had. Stick, a lifetime .229 hitter with a .288 on-base percentage, was obsessed with players getting on base long before the 2003 book *Moneyball* portrayed Billy Beane as the patron saint of that approach. Naturally, part of getting on base is taking pitches, spoiling pitches, and forcing pitchers to throw strikes.

"It seemed like when we got Boggs here and he was wearing out pitchers and having elevated pitch counts in his at-bats, I felt like his approach had a domino effect throughout the rest of our lineup," said Brian Cashman, who was an assistant GM under Michael. "He's a perennial batting champion–type and people followed him. So I feel like it kind of started with Boggs. And we just kind of got better at it and imported more people like that along the way."

Not only did Michael change the culture around the Yankees and help transform them into the best team in the American League during the strike-shortened 1994 and into a postseason team in 1995, he also protected and nurtured the Yankees' premier prospects. Bernie Williams debuted in 1991 and, at times, looked uncertain and fragile, a skinny kid with gold-framed glasses who was still learning how to be a major leaguer. But Michael would tell Yankee officials and reporters that he envisioned Williams blossoming into an excellent hitter who would provide both power and speed. And Stick was willing to be patient and wait for Williams to become that player.

"He was instrumental for me," Williams said. "And, if I didn't have that backing of someone who was so high in the organization and who was rooting for me and was letting me struggle with my growing pains, I don't think I would have been able to stay on the team as long as I did."

Any time Steinbrenner grew impatient with Williams and suggested to Michael that the Yankees include him in a trade, which happened multiple times, Michael quickly and cleverly rebuffed the Boss.

The Joy of Jeter

"I heard stories about him misleading George Steinbrenner a little bit and making him believe nobody wanted me when some people in the organization wanted to trade me," Williams said, with a laugh. "So that meant they were stuck with me! I heard a lot of stories like that and they make me feel great and appreciated. They let me develop into the player I would become and I'm grateful for that."

Every Yankee fan should be grateful for Williams and grateful that the Yankees let him develop. Because Williams developed into such a stellar performer, the Yankees were more patient with the young players who followed him: Mariano Rivera, Andy Pettitte, Jeter, and Posada, who became known as the Core Four and who were significant factors in the Yankees winning four championships in five seasons. All four players have credited Williams for making a perilous path much less perilous for them. Rivera and Pettitte followed Williams to the majors in 1995. Jeter, after playing briefly with the Yankees in 1995, became the starting shortstop in 1996 and Posada, who played in nine games for the Yankees in 1995 and 1996, was a contributor in the majors for good by 1997. And, by 1998, Williams and Jeter and Posada were part of a lineup that was terrorizing pitchers in a way that amazed Jeter. The Yankees were second in the major leagues in seeing 3.85 pitches per plate appearance. Oakland was first at 3.92.

"You would know better than me, but I think the 1998 Yankees really started the conversation of players getting on base and working counts and getting starting pitchers to 100 pitches because you really didn't hear much of that before then," Jeter said. "But we would just wear pitchers down. There were guys who had 100 pitches through four or five innings because we didn't swing at too many bad pitches, we worked counts, we'd take our walks, and we fouled pitches off. We were pests at the plate and that was all of us, from one through nine."

There were so many snapshots from the 1998 season, so many positive and celebratory images as the Yankees steamrolled teams. At one point, the Yankees went 24 straight series without losing one. They also had a lead in 48 straight games. But, in reviewing countless hours of footage from that season, it was apparent how often Jeter was the first Yankee to congratulate a teammate after the player smacked a homer or scored a run. It was intentional and it stemmed from Jeter's Little League days.

As a 10-year-old Little Leaguer in Kalamazoo, young Derek was so disappointed by a loss that he refused to shake the opponent's hands. After Charles Jeter, Derek's father, noticed this, he delivered a life lesson, one that benefited the Yankees years later.

"My dad told me, 'You'd better pick an individual sport' to play because you have to be there for your teammates through good times and in bad times," Jeter remembered. "That's why when you saw me throughout the course of my career I was always at the top step and was one of the first to congratulate one of my teammates."

Congratulate every teammate? Yes. Get along perfectly with every teammate? Not always. Although Jeter said the 1998 team was egoless, that doesn't mean all of the players were best buddies. A clubhouse is home to splendid athletes and men who are among the best in the world at what they do. But, like any workplace environment, an employee might not always like the colleague who is in another office.

Jeter didn't specifically remember a teammate chastising another teammate, but added, "I'm sure it probably happened." When I told Jeter a few teammates noted that he and outfielder Chad Curtis used to argue over the music choices in the clubhouse, Jeter quickly acknowledged that was true.

"Oh, yeah," Jeter said. "So that answers your question. It wasn't like no one ever got into it. I used to get into it with him quite a lot."

With a close-cropped haircut, serious eyes, and a monotone voice, Curtis was a player who liked to read the Bible by his locker and who also liked to proselytize to his teammates. Some were receptive as Curtis attended a daily prayer group with several other Yankees. But some others were not as receptive. Jeter, who turned 24 in June 1998, favored music by artists like Jay-Z. The New York–born rapper, who boasted that "I made a Yankee hat more famous than a Yankee can," also included profanities in his lyrics. Curtis didn't like hearing those words. So he and Jeter bickered.

"For the most part, I would say that team was drama-free," said Mike Buddie, a rookie reliever. "I remember Jeter and Chad Curtis getting into arguments over the music choices in the locker room. Jeter liked contemporary hip-hop and Chad didn't like anything that had a choice word in it."

Despite the music squabbles, Jeter coexisted with Curtis. Remember, it was Jeter who confronted Wells on behalf of himself, Curtis, and Ledée when the pop fly ball dropped between the three Yankees. Jeter didn't have to agree about music lyrics in order to be a good teammate.

Jeter lived in Manhattan during his career so he routinely

interacted with fans. The more that Jeter's stature grew, the more frequent and the more boisterous those interactions became. Everyone wanted a piece of Jeter, even if it was just to say a quick hello, to tell him they had a number 2 jersey, or to imitate his batting stance. The selfie had not yet become commonplace or Jeter might still be stranded on the Upper East Side. Actually, Jeter was so adept at being able to acknowledge fans and move on with his plans that he would have conquered any obstacles.

But, on one afternoon in early September, Jeter was jolted by something a fan said. The Yankees were about 100–40 at this point, they were entrenched in first place, and the post-season beckoned. The Yankees were in a stretch in which they sputtered and lost nine of 15 games to start the month, but they were still on an incredible pace. It was just a blip and special things were still ahead of them, Jeter thought. But at least one skeptical New Yorker felt differently and expressed himself loudly.

"I remember this like it was yesterday," Jeter said. "I was either going to get something to eat or I was going to my car to drive to the stadium. And, remember, we had pretty much clinched the division in about April. And here we are in September and I remember this guy coming up to me and he wasn't joking and he said, 'You'd better turn it around.' And he was almost angry. And, while I remember him, he wasn't the only one who thought that way. And that only happens in New York. And that's why you've got to love playing here."

As laser-focused as Jeter typically was, he had allowed himself to delve into bad habits in search of a homer. When

Jeter homered for the second time on September 9, it was his 19th of the season in the team's 143rd game. He was also batting .334 at the time. For some reason, Jeter, who had never hit more than 10 homers and never considered himself a home run hitter, had visions of Nomar Garciaparra and A-Rod in his head and he started to chase the long ball. He desperately wanted to collect his 20th homer.

With his ability to wait on the baseball, Jeter was at his best when he was attacking and hitting baseballs to the opposite field. But he was a different hitter across the final three weeks, going 18 for 72 (.250) and never hitting that elusive 20th homer. Instead of continuing to spray line drives around the field, Jeter tried to hit the ball out of the park. And that wasn't him. It was a valuable reminder for Jeter because he steered away from the things that made him a superb hitter. The slump cost Jeter a chance to challenge Williams for the batting title, which Williams won with a .339 average. Jeter hit .324, scored an American League high 127 runs, and finished third in the MVP voting behind Juan González and Garciaparra. And, of course, he also finished with 19 homers.

"I learned a lot from that period," Jeter said. "It's nice to set some goals and 20 homers would have been great, but I shouldn't have done it at the expense of changing who I was as a hitter."

Whether Jeter was hitting in a game or before a game, he was always confident and always competitive. During batting practice, the Yankees would have a hitting competition called "the RBI game." Each hitter in a three-batter group would imagine he was up with the bases loaded and one out.

For every fly ball, line drive, grounder, or pop-up, the players would earn points for hits or lose points for outs.

"When Jeter played in his hitting group," Girardi said, "he won the game a lot."

But, being both playful and challenging, Jeter would repeatedly quiz Girardi about the title of this competition.

"What's this game called?" Jeter would ask.

"It's the RBI game," Girardi would say.

Jeter would pause before declaring, "I win. That's the name of the game."

And, quite often, Jeter did win.

"That exchange always stuck with me," Girardi said. "He would ask the name of the game and then he'd say, 'I win' was the name. He just had that confidence in anything he did. Jete was as competitive as any player that I was ever around. That's just who he was."

The baseball season is a long season, a long and grueling season, and a lot of that season is spent inside a clubhouse. When the players aren't working on their craft, some listen to music, some do crossword puzzles, some play cards, some tease their teammates, and some read to pass the time. And some, like Jeter, play board games.

Connect 4 is a two-person board game that is advertised as being for ages six and older and it was very popular among the Yankees. Jeter loved to play the game against Scott Brosius. Hours away from facing an assortment of fastballs, sliders, and curveballs, Jeter and Brosius found comfort and a new way to compete in a board game that was born in 1974, the same year as Jeter. Before Jeter and Brosius jogged out to the field to cover the left side of the infield and play a kid's game, they played another kid's game in the clubhouse. And, sometimes, they shouted more passionately about a win in Connect 4 than they did about a run-scoring single.

"There are different personalities and different people in a clubhouse," Jeter said. "With some guys, you can yell and scream at them. With some guys, you got to give them hugs. But you've got to know who you're leading. I always prided myself on getting to know my teammates. It doesn't necessarily mean you have to go to dinner with them every night, but you need to take the time to know him."

And Brosius and Jeter, as valuable as any position players on the 1998 team, got to know each other while playing Connect 4.

"I would dominate," Jeter said. "Please write that in the book. I would dominate Scott Brosius in Connect 4. Other people would try and come in and play, but it was mainly me and Scott. And I would dominate."

Dominate. Just like the 1998 Yankees.

CHAPTER 6

Start Spreading the News

Disneyland is the happiest place on Earth. Right? Many of us have been to Disneyland in Anaheim and many others have at least seen the promotions that tell us how wonderful it is. Delighted visitors get the chance to see Mickey Mouse, scream and screech through some rides, and gawk at a parade, all while telling themselves it truly is a magical spot. Right?

For Scott Brosius, Disneyland was the unlikely setting for a magical change, a career pivot that helped him achieve his ultimate dream of winning a World Series title. But there's no way Brosius expected an innocuous day in November 1997 to be remembered as one of the most impactful of his baseball life. That would have been far-fetched. Not even Disneyland, the happiest of happy places, was supposed to be the launching point for such a compelling journey.

After an abysmal season in which he hit .203 with the Oakland A's, Brosius and his family were vacationing at Disneyland. He anticipated soon being traded. Since Brosius had heard speculation that he might be moved to the Angels, he and his wife, Jennifer, joked about simply staying in Mickey's neighborhood if the trade happened while they were in Anaheim. As Brosius recounted the details to Sweeny Murti of WFAN radio, he said, "This is perfect. I'm here. We don't have to go anywhere."

Upon returning to his room from the hotel pool, Brosius noticed that Jennifer was on the phone. When she said nothing and passed him the phone, Brosius knew that he had been traded. Tony Attanasio, his agent, was on the other end of the line.

"Where am I going?" Brosius asked Attanasio.

Attanasio didn't speak. He sang.

"Da da da daaa, Da! Da da da daaa, Da!" Attanasio bellowed. And Attanasio proceeded with the lyrics of "New York, New York" by singing, "Start spreading the news…" Brosius knew Frank Sinatra's iconic song and knew Ol' Blue Eyes crooned, "I want to be a part of it: New York, New York."

Even still, Brosius told Murti he wasn't sure where he had been traded.

"I thought he was joking because all of our conversations were about anywhere but New York," Brosius said. "The Yankees were not in it. So I said, 'Really, where am I going?'"

Attanasio, the full-time agent and part-time karaoke singer, started singing Sinatra again. So Brosius was now convinced he was heading to New York, but he didn't know if he was going to the Yankees or the Mets. Finally, Attanasio told him, "You got traded to the Yankees!"

Standing in a hotel room in the land of Mickey and Minnie with an agent playing a version of *Name That Tune*. That was the goofy way Brosius started his career in New York and began his surprising ascent to a prominent place on the 1998 Yankees and in franchise history.

While interviewing several dozen people about the 1998 Yankees, some of the first names mentioned were always Derek Jeter, Bernie Williams, Mariano Rivera, David Cone, Paul O'Neill, and Joe Torre. But Brosius's name was cited just as often and just as passionately. In searching for reasons why the 1998 Yankees were remarkable, it's shrewd to start with the fact that Brosius, who was a menace at the bottom of the order, had a glorious and unexpected season. He hit .300 with a .371 on-base percentage, a .472 slugging percentage, 19 homers and 98 runs batted in. Plus, Brosius played a Gold Glove–caliber defense that left some of his teammates in awe.

"Brosius was probably as underrated a player as you could have on that team," Jeter said. "And it sounds kind of funny to say it because he was the World Series MVP. But Brosius was a guy who came up with clutch hits for us and was consistent in the field. And he was a fun guy to play with."

And let's be candid about the trade involving Brosius and pitcher Kenny Rogers: As integral as Brosius wound up being, the deal was originally viewed as a salary dump by the Yankees. The Yankees had been trying to unload the misplaced Rogers for more than a year and they succeeded by dealing him for Brosius, who had just had the worst season of his career. To finalize the deal, the Yankees agreed to absorb $5 million of the $10 million left on Rogers's contract.

Since the A's were required to protect Brosius in the expansion draft as part of the deal, the Yankees only announced they had acquired a player to be named later, although reporters ferreted out that it was Brosius. Eleven days after the agreement was hatched, the Yankees officially disclosed Brosius was the player. But the news was treated so inconsequentially that the Yankees never had a conference call to introduce Brosius to the New York media.

In my story about Brosius in the *New York Times*, I called him a utility player because that is what he had been in 1997. Brosius started 78 of the A's first 96 games at third base, but then started only 16 games at third the rest of the season. He also played shortstop and all three outfield positions. Soon after the deal, Jon Heyman, who was a respected columnist for *Newsday*, wrote about how the Yankees and Mets had been unsuccessful in adding marquee players in the off-season: "Yet neither team has added one significant player—unless one counts Scott Brosius." The sarcasm was heavy, but so was the realism. Brosius wasn't considered a high-profile addition.

After hitting .304 with 22 homers in 1996, Brosius plummeted in 1997. Really plummeted. While he continued to play exemplary defense, Brosius's batting average dropped 101 points and his slugging percentage decreased by 199 points. He also had arthroscopic knee surgery. During the 1998 postseason, Brosius actually said it might be harder to hit .200 than .300, which was his way of saying how unfortunate and how unlucky he had been in 1997. He hit .165 on the road, a major league worst.

What did the Yankees see in the struggling Brosius?

Well, it wasn't the Yankees who were looking, per se. It was Ron Brand, their West Coast scout. General Manager Bob

Watson had assigned Brian Cashman, his assistant, the job of being the liaison to about half of the teams in the majors. When the Yankees communicated with those teams, Cashman handled it. The A's were one of those teams. So Cashman dealt with Billy Beane, Oakland's GM, but Cashman accepted the most input from Brand.

"I had Ron Brand in my ear," Cashman said, "telling me how much he believed in Brosius."

The Yankees had declined Wade Boggs's $2 million option and they were intent on shedding Charlie Hayes, later paying his entire salary and shipping him to the San Francisco Giants. They were hunting for a third baseman. Brand told Cashman that Brosius had the talent to be the starting third baseman and, at the very least, could be a solid utility player who could play any position except catcher. The deal was struck. Yankee fans yawned.

With Brosius taking over third base in a new and pressure-filled city, Torre had a plan: Brosius needed to play a lot to become acclimated to New York and for Torre to gauge exactly what type of player he was. With Jeter, Chuck Knoblauch, and Tino Martinez also entrenched in the infield, Torre told backup infielder Luis Sojo that he shouldn't expect to play much early in the season. But everyone knew Jeter, Knoblauch, and Martinez were expected to play a lot. This strategy was about testing and scrutinizing Brosius. And it worked.

Brosius started the first 10 games, took one game off, and started 32 of the next 34 games (and played in one of the two games he didn't start). He took a shocking two games off and then started the next 32 straight games. Brosius rested in Game 81. But, at the midway point of the season, Brosius had played in 77 games and was already a mainstay on a team that was an astounding 61–20. Brosius had played in more games than any other infielder and had grown quite comfortable in his new environment.

"This is not meant to be a knock on Oakland, but when you come to the ballpark and there are only 7,000 fans, it takes on a minor league atmosphere," Brosius told *Newsday*. "When you come here and fans are up on their feet applauding for a strikeout in the second or third inning, it's the type of place and atmosphere that a player enjoys."

At first, Torre put Brosius in the lineup almost every day because he needed answers about Brosius as a player. But, before too long, Torre had those answers and he kept playing Brosius on a daily basis because Brosius was one of the most valuable players on the team.

"You want to find out what you have," Torre said. "With New York, even when I wasn't working for the Yankees, I observed how certain players could handle it and how other players couldn't handle it. I wanted to see for myself. And I never could have dreamed the package that we would get in Bro. He did everything well. He was remarkable."

Every player wants to make a positive impression with a new team and, if possible, it's even more critical to make that impression quickly. Despite Brosius playing 606 games across seven seasons in Oakland, some Yankees admitted they weren't overly familiar with all of his abilities. But the soft-spoken Brosius asserted himself swiftly, especially on defense. He had superb instincts, quick feet, excellent lateral movement, and an arm that was reliable, so reliable and so true.

"Ask Tino about Brosius throwing the ball across the diamond," catcher Jorge Posada said. "It was always right at his chest. There was never a ball that Tino had to pick. Brosius always threw four-seamers to Tino's chest. You never saw him throwing the ball away."

Naturally, I took Posada's advice and asked Tino about Brosius's arm.

"He threw strikes to first every single time," Martinez said. "When he joined us that year, I didn't know he was that good. His range and his arm were incredible."

The player who was positioned closest to Brosius was Jeter and the shortstop soon realized he was watching a skilled defender. Before Jeter and Brosius became combatants who played Connect 4 in the clubhouse, Jeter marveled at how smooth and aggressive Brosius was at third.

"Brosius was unbelievable as a defensive player," Jeter said. "I didn't know much about Scott. We played them a couple of times a year. So I didn't know much about him before he came over, but I was shocked at how good he was defensively."

In a career that started with a cup of coffee in 1995 and ended with glory in 2014, Jeter never played any position except shortstop for the Yankees. While Jeter was playing 2,674 games at short, he looked to his right at 66 different third basemen. That list included Álex Rodríguez, who won two MVPs with the Yankees and had previously won two Gold Gloves as a shortstop, and Boggs, a future Hall of Famer who won two Gold Gloves as a Yankee, and Hayes, a player whose rotund physique belied how dependable he was as a fielder. But Brosius, cool and steady, was atop that list of 66.

"Derek thought Brosius was probably the best defensive third baseman he ever played with," Posada said. "And that says a lot."

But that didn't mean Brosius caught everything. On April 29, Ken Griffey Jr. hit a soft fly ball into shallow left field at Yankee Stadium. It should have been an out and a sigh of relief for starting pitcher David Cone because Griffey was such a lethal hitter. But Brosius drifted about a dozen steps onto the outfield grass, seemed to be off-balance, reached to his left to make the catch, and had the ball bounce off the heel of his glove. An unearned run scored and the miscue fueled the Mariners to a 3–0 lead.

"That's just a concentration error there," said Ray Knight, the ESPN analyst and former third baseman who was broadcasting the game. "That's just a routine play for any major league player."

The fans felt the same way.

"And the crowd is going, 'Go back to Oakland. Who are you?'" Brosius told WFAN's Murti.

Who are you? That stung, even though Cone and the Yankees won that game, 8–5. For the next few weeks, Jeter seized control and essentially froze out Brosius by calling him off virtually every pop-up to the left side of the infield.

"And I would look over at him like, 'Dude, are you going to let me catch a pop-up again or what?'" Brosius recalled. "And he had a smile. He would call me off of balls where I was standing right under them, which he has a right to do as a shortstop.

It just became this ongoing thing where I was like, 'Dude, are you ever going to let me catch a ball again?'"

The answer to that question, Brosius found out, was yes. As Brosius told Murti, it was done with a bit of humor.

"So now this ball is hit and maybe he should take it and maybe I should take it," Brosius explained. "And I'm going back toward left field and I'm calling, like I'm always trying to do. And I don't hear him calling me off. I don't hear anything. So I'm like, 'He's going to let me catch it.' And, just as I'm catching it, he goes, 'AHHHHHHH,' and tries to scare me. I looked at him and said, 'Dude, are you serious?' And he just took the ball and threw it around. It was that kind of thing when he was on the field. It was always about winning, but he also enjoyed playing too. And I think you have to have that love for the competition."

For Brosius, the love of competition started at the age of three when he said he dreamed of being a baseball player. Born in Milwaukie, Oregon, Brosius played three sports in high school and was guided by Maury, his Mickey Mantle–loving father. But Oregon is a long way, literally and figuratively, from the major leagues. In fact, Brosius didn't see his first big-league game until he was an A's minor leaguer and his Single-A team played before an Oakland-Milwaukee game. During the A's game, Brosius hung out in the left field seats and caught a home run ball. Brosius told *Newsday* he declined to give the ball to a kid.

"It's my first game too," he explained.

Still, regardless of where Brosius was born and raised or where he started his professional career, he was the picture of comfort in the Bronx.

"There was an easiness about his personality that allowed him to fit in so well," Cone said. "He seemed so relieved to be out of Oakland. It seemed like the pressure was off. He was going to bat ninth and play good defense at third. It was like he felt renewed. You could sense it. He was relaxed when he came to New York. It's kind of odd when you think about it when you go from a small market in Oakland to New York. You would think it would be the other way around. But it wasn't. He fit in perfectly."

Perfectly and immediately. Brosius drove in four runs against his old friends from Oakland as the Yankees outlasted the A's, 17–13, in their home opener on April 10. Less than two weeks later, Brosius stared down Roger Clemens and socked three hits and knocked in five runs as the Yankees squashed Toronto, 9–1. Clemens would win his fifth Cy Young that season and get traded to the Yankees in 1999. One day after the Yankees stopped the Rocket, Brosius rapped three hits in an 8–4 win over the Tigers. But Brosius really soared in May as he hit .396 with three homers and 17 RBIs in 25 games, cementing his status as a linchpin player and pushing himself toward the All-Star Game.

"You want to talk about big hits," Jeter said, "he had big hits all the way through the World Series."

And Brosius did make his first All-Star team. It seemed somewhat fitting that the Yankees, who were a team with some blossoming stars and no superstars (yet), didn't have any players voted to start in the game. But five Yankees made the American League team as reserves: Brosius, Jeter, O'Neill, Williams, and David Wells.

Interestingly enough, Brosius's first All-Star at-bat came against Trevor Hoffman, the goateed San Diego closer with the parachute changeup. At that time, that was just another at-bat in an exhibition game between the National League and the American League. Three months later, an at-bat between them would end with a Brosius three-run homer that helped decide Game 3 of the World Series. But, on this night, Hoffman ruled. Brosius fouled off two fastballs and a changeup, and then stared at a beautiful changeup that caught the outside corner. Fortunately for Brosius, Hoffman wouldn't have that same nasty changeup in October, but we will dive into that story in Chapter 9.

Serious and seasoned, John Flaherty was a catcher for the 1998 Tampa Bay Devil Rays. Expansion teams are supposed to lose a lot. While Flaherty understood that reality, he was devoted to developing the best game plans to squelch an offense. The Rays were 63–99 that season, but Flaherty's job was to find a batter's weakness and try to help his pitchers exploit it.

That sounded like a smart approach, but, against the 1998 Yankees, it was fairly futile. There weren't many weaknesses to attack in the deep Yankees' lineup because their talented hitters were also tenacious and patient. The Yankees fouled off pitches, they didn't swing at pitches that were inches off the plate, and they waited for strikes. If pitchers didn't throw strikes, the Yankees' batters would accept a walk and let a teammate do the damage.

"It was draining," Flaherty said.

Flaherty, who grew up in West Nyack, New York, as a Thurman Munson fan and later played with the Yankees from 2003 to 2005, said that most teams have a soft landing spot in the lower third of the lineup. OK, Flaherty might say to his pitchers, you fought through those first seven hitters, but now there's a couple of easier outs at the bottom of the order. With the Yankees, those easier outs didn't exist.

"And that was because of Brosius," Flaherty said. "You'd pitch to Derek, Bernie, and O'Neill and you'd think you'd have a place to catch your breath a bit. And you look up and Brosius is at the plate. When I think about that team, he's actually the first guy I think about."

Jeff Nelson, an astute reliever who watched the game like a scout, agreed.

"I think the 1998 team was probably the best team in the history of baseball," Nelson said. "Look at who we had hitting one through nine. We had Brosius hitting eighth and ninth and he had 98 RBIs. That team battled pitchers. They'd foul pitches off and they'd get into deep counts. They weren't afraid to hit with two strikes. That was one of the main recipes for success in 1998. They just wore down pitchers."

Examples of this ferocious approach littered the Yankees' schedule, with pitcher's arms and earned runs averages getting bludgeoned.

On May 6, the Yankees defeated the Rangers, 15–13. Starter Bobby Witt threw 48 pitches and allowed seven runs in one and one-third innings. Tim Crabtree followed Witt and tossed 54 pitches while giving up four runs in one and two-third innings.

On May 24, the Yankees battered the Red Sox, 14–4. Bret Saberhagen uncorked 71 pitches while surrendering half of those runs and not lasting through the third inning. The next pitcher and the next victim was Ron Mahay and he was torched for five runs and needed 73 pitches to get though two innings.

Even when the Yankees lost, they made pitchers earn the win. That included the best pitchers too. Pedro Martínez and the Red Sox stifled the Yankees, 13–7, on May 31. But Martínez, who had been given an 11-run lead in the third, threw a whopping 130 pitches in five innings.

Finally, the man who is least likely to buy this book is Mike Oquist of the A's because he had the pitching line from hell against the lineup from hell. In a 14–1 loss on August 3, Oquist was shellacked for 14 runs on 16 hits in a five-inning, 115-pitch stint. It was the most runs allowed by a pitcher since 1977. With a doubleheader scheduled for the next day, Manager Art Howe needed Oquist to supply some innings and take one for the team. Howe said he was "bleeding" with Oquist. More like hemorrhaging.

"Every one of those guys in their lineup is a good hitter," Oquist told reporters. "They take a lot of pitches and they're going to wait for the one they like. I just tried to keep going after them." He added, "I've never really been hit like that before."

Oquist had been teammates with Brosius, but on that day and in that season, they were on opposite ends of the baseball world. Even though Brand's scouting report inspired the Yankees to engineer a trade for Brosius, they wanted some insurance in case Brosius faltered. Since the Yankees decided minor leaguer Mike Lowell, a future World Series MVP with the 2007 Red Sox, wasn't yet ready for the majors, New York signed Dale Sveum to a two-year, $1.6 million deal.

"Everyone wants to play for the Yankees," Sveum said.

So did Sveum. But he hardly ever played. Brosius started almost every day and he produced, leaving few at-bats for Sveum. Rookie teammates Homer Bush and Mike Buddie both praised Sveum for how helpful and instructive he was, but Sveum wanted to play and those opportunities barely existed. He started twice in the first 33 games of the season and had only 48 plate appearances at the All-Star Game break.

"As the season wore on, I thought to myself, 'Unless there's an injury here, I'm not going to play a whole lot,'" Sveum said. "Those guys were playing every day and they were really good and they were having really good years."

Since Sveum knew he was the "25th guy on the roster," he said he showed up to work every day wondering if he might lose his roster spot. Eventually, he did. On July 27, the Yankees recalled Shane Spencer from Triple-A and designated Sveum for assignment. He had a guarantee of more than $1 million left on his contract.

"The sad thing about getting released is knowing, 'Holy shit, I'm not going to be part of the playoffs and a final run and a very, very good chance of being in the World Series,'" Sveum said. "And I'd never been in the playoffs as a player. That was the most disappointing thing that happened."

But a shocking and revealing thing happened on Sveum's way out the door: He remained with the Yankees as a bullpen catcher and a batting practice pitcher. Yes, an active player on a wildly successful team basically went from taking batting practice to throwing batting practice and handling other support roles. Since Joe Girardi had a sore knee, Sveum had been catching bullpen sessions to save Girardi from the extra work. When Sveum cleared waivers and no team attempted to sign him, he stayed in a Yankee uniform.

"Joe Torre asked me if I wanted to stay on and do that role," Sveum said. "Well, since nobody wanted me, I just stayed on and caught bullpens, threw some BP in the cage, and hit fungoes."

While Sveum hadn't been an instrumental part of the Yankees because of his scant playing time, it was incredibly rare for a player to shift into a support role in the same season. But this was the 1998 Yankees. Something special was happening. The gracious Sveum even invited Spencer, the man who took his roster spot, to live in his apartment.

"Obviously, if we were in last place, I probably would have gone home," Sveum said. "I had never been in the playoffs. And, even though I wasn't going to experience it as a player, I did experience it from the sidelines. I knew it was an experience I might never be around again. You never know if you'll be around a postseason team again. At that time, I thought it would be a very cool experience."

Another first-year Yankee was Darren Holmes, a rugged and thoughtful pitcher who had signed a three-year, $4.65 million free agent contract. After eight seasons with the Los Angeles Dodgers, the Colorado Rockies, and the Milwaukee Brewers, Holmes brought a curveball he learned from the legendary Sandy Koufax to the Bronx. He remembered a conversation he had with a New York reporter about life as a Yankee.

"How is it going to feel to wear the pinstripes and be a Yankee?" the reporter asked.

Holmes started to answer casually and said, "I've played against the Yankees quite a few times at home and on the road."

And the reporter interrupted him.

"But," he said, "you've never played there in pinstripes."

That comment jolted Holmes and was a reminder of how much pressure there is while pitching in New York, something he felt. When Holmes had a 13.50 ERA in his first four games as a Yankee, principal owner George Steinbrenner said, "We've got to have it out of the young man from Colorado. I didn't know anything about him when we signed him. My baseball people took care of that. They say he throws 95 miles per hour. I want to see it." The criticism emboldened Holmes, who agreed with the Boss. "He was right," Holmes said. "I wasn't performing to my level."

Eventually, Holmes performed to his level. He allowed one earned run in his last 11 games and narrowly missed being included on the postseason roster. But Holmes also experienced what it was like to fizzle and be the target of Yankee fans. Every time players walked into Yankee Stadium, fans would be lined up behind metal barriers and they would offer encouragement to some players or deride some players. For the first month of the season, Holmes said there was one obnoxious fan who barked at him every day and called him a disappointment.

Finally, in an 8–6 win over the Texas Rangers on May 13, Holmes entered in the eighth inning and retired Juan González on a pop out to shortstop and Will Clark on a fly ball to left field. González and Clark would finish their careers with 718 homers and 4,112 hits, so this was clearly Holmes's biggest test as a Yankee. As Holmes walked off the mound, he received a warm ovation. Mariano Rivera notched the final four outs for the save. Still, there was one final part of Holmes's test that night.

"When I walked to the parking lot, the same guy who had worn me out daily yelled to me and he said, 'Welcome! You're now a Yankee,'" Holmes recalled. "Every time I think about that and every time I tell the story, I get goose bumps because he was right. I was a Yankee. I hadn't yet proven myself to be a Yankee. I think that one game with Texas made me a Yankee. From then on, it was a lot of fun."

Fun is a word that could sometimes be associated with Paul O'Neill, but only after he had smacked a few hits. Or maybe a few dozen hits. Ornery and intense, O'Neill was one of the symbols of that 1998 team. Shockingly, O'Neill never believed that a pitcher had retired him. He always believed that he had made the out. Since O'Neill had surely notched a hit against the same type of pitch that just retired him, he never wanted to give a pitcher any credit. It was an absurd theory, but it's what O'Neill believed and what drove him. And Holmes learned a lot by simply observing O'Neill.

Holmes and O'Neill usually carpooled from their homes in Westchester County to the stadium. On the drive home after a game in April, Holmes asked O'Neill what time he wanted to leave for the Bronx the next day. It was an off day before a road trip and the players were required to arrive by 1:30 p.m. to take a bus to the airport.

"Let's leave at 9:30," O'Neill told Holmes.

Holmes was taken aback by the early departure time and said, "Hey O, our bus doesn't leave until 1:30."

"Holmesy," O'Neill said, "nothing changes about what I have to do tomorrow. We're just not playing a ball game. I still have to lift, I still have to throw, I still have to hit, I still have to get treatment, and I still have to work out. I still have the same routine."

A curious Holmes nodded and said nothing. And, when Holmes and O'Neill sauntered into the clubhouse by about 10:15 a.m. the next day, Holmes discovered that other Yankees shared the same work ethic and same philosophy as O'Neill.

"There were a lot of players who were already there and that shook me a little bit," Holmes said. "It was one of the early signs of how great this organization was, how devoted the players were, and how they bought into what we were trying to do. And I just happened to be a part of it."

What Holmes witnessed said a lot about the Yankees. But at least Holmes managed to get a ride with O'Neill. There were times where O'Neill left Knoblauch stranded. It had nothing to do with Knoblauch. It had everything to do with O'Neill.

"As quiet as O'Neill was off the field, he was nuts on the field," Knoblauch said. "As soon as we got in the clubhouse after a game, he would say, 'I can't give you a ride home today because I went 0 for 4.' I was like, 'OK Paul. No worries. My bad.'"

And then Knoblauch laughed at O'Neill's anger and superstition.

"He didn't want to talk to anybody," Knoblauch said. "Not me anyway. I think he might have blamed me for going 0 for 4 and thought I was the bad luck charm. I don't know. It was funny."

Even if O'Neill's refusal to give Knoblauch a ride was comical, his focused, manic, and driven approach was instrumental to his success. Don Mattingly, the former Yankees' captain, described O'Neill as "the main guy in turning it around for the Yankees" after he was acquired from the Reds before the 1993 season. Mattingly said O'Neill "wouldn't settle" for simply being ordinary and "nothing was good enough." And, according to Girardi, O'Neill's passion impacted his teammates too.

"Paul O'Neill gets credit for being a great player and a great Yankee," said Girardi. "But I don't think he gets enough credit for what his attitude did for our clubhouse every day. It wasn't good enough to just have one or two good at-bats. Paul wanted to have four good at-bats a day and do everything he could to help us win a game. Paul had that desire for perfection that I think a lot of players have. But Paul's came out and we saw it. That rubbed off on the team. There was a sense of urgency every day because you felt it so much from Paul O'Neill."

Looking stoic and Buddha-like from his dugout perch, Torre never disclosed his emotions to his players, which was intentional. But he was constantly impressed by them as 1998

unfolded. After Torre reminded the Yankees they had "unfinished business" in spring training and after he upbraided them less than a week into the season during a meeting in Seattle, he managed a team that was machinelike.

"That ball club came to spring training so determined that they left stuff on the table in '97," Torre said. "And I really never realized how determined they were until they refused to make the idea of not winning a game so important. I feel like I pulled them into spring training and just jumped on their backs and enjoyed the ride."

Over and over, the players discussed Torre's importance to what the Yankees accomplished in 1998. Surely, one could ask the question: How hard was it to manage a team that is in the discussion for the best team of all time? Even Torre would surely admit that's a valid question. But the players disagreed.

"We would never die," Posada said. "We always thought we could win. We came to the stadium every day knowing we had a chance to win the game. But the key to all of it was probably Joe Torre. He kept everything so even-keeled."

Andy Pettitte concurred with Posada.

"Joe never panicked in any situation," Pettitte said. "With his personality, we fed off that. He was kind of low-key and, as long as we were professional and doing what we needed to do, he was always encouraging to all of us."

Jeter summed it up similarly.

"He never lost his cool," Jeter said. "There were times where we had meetings and he would get upset and he would yell and scream. And then it was done. He was calm. I still think he was the perfect manager for what we were going through.

As the smart and soothing manager of the Yankees, **JOE TORRE** was a comforting presence in the dugout. Players praised Torre for never panicking and for always being in control. They also lauded Torre for holding a meeting in the first week of the season that helped spark the team. Derek Jeter called Torre "the perfect manager" for the 1998 Yankees.

GEORGE STEINBRENNER didn't mind pointing fingers to emphasize how much he wanted players to produce and how much he wanted the Yankees to win. After the Yankees lost to Cleveland in the 1997 postseason, the principal owner stood in the losing clubhouse and guaranteed the Yankees would win it all in 1998. He was right.

For one glorious afternoon in May, **DAVID WELLS** was flawless as he pitched a perfect game against the Twins. An eager Wells stared toward right field and waited for Paul O'Neill to catch Pat Meares's fly ball for the 27th and final out. Despite starting the game with a hangover, Wells became the 15th pitcher in history to toss a perfect game.

ORLANDO "EL DUQUE" HERNÁNDEZ was a mystery man from Cuba, a pitcher who was talented and fearless. He won the most crucial game of the season when he tamed Cleveland in the American League Championship Series. With a distinctive motion in which his left leg almost touched his chin, El Duque was so cool and so confident.

Creative, intelligent, and driven, **DAVID CONE** was a superb pitcher and a great teammate. After pondering retirement early in April, Cone rebounded to win 20 games and formed a dynamic duo with David Wells on and off the field. Cone, who was the ultimate New York baseball player, called the 1998 Yankees the best constructed roster in history.

After **JORGE POSADA** caught David Wells's perfect game, Wells said that Posada was "perfect," too, because Wells never shook off any of Posada's signs. Posada also counseled Orlando Hernández after Hernández arrived from Cuba. The fiery Posada was one of the players who most epitomized the Yankees' grinding approach.

Dashing up the first base line, **PAUL O'NEILL** looked like he was chasing another hit. Because he surely was. Another hit. Another line drive. Another win. O'Neill was always pursuing perfection, which made him the intense and successful player that he was. His passionate approach earned him the nickname "The Warrior" from owner George Steinbrenner.

After **BERNIE WILLIAMS** made the final out of the 1997 postseason, he was morose. Williams vowed to work incredibly hard in the off-season and be more prepared than ever before. And he was. Williams flourished in 1998 as he won the American League batting title and ignored the distractions of his impending free agency.

SHANE SPENCER was a career minor leaguer who became the most dangerous hitter for the Yankees in September. The Yankees dominated baseball for five months and didn't seem to need any upgrades, but Spencer forced his way into the party with some prodigious swings in the final month of the regular season. He was "The Natural."

With a sweet swing, **DARRYL STRAWBERRY** was a joy to watch at the plate. He blasted 24 homers in a part-time role. Strawberry played through considerable pain before learning he had colon cancer during the first round of the playoffs. He wasn't able to participate in the postseason, but the Yankees chanted Strawberry's name in the clubhouse after winning it all in San Diego.

CHUCK KNOBLAUCH defiantly tossed his bat after clubbing a three-run homer off Donne Wall to tie the score in Game 1 of the World Series. Ten days after Knoblauch had failed to chase a loose baseball against Cleveland in the playoffs and was excoriated for his brain cramp, Knoblauch said he felt some redemption after the homer.

TINO MARTINEZ pumped his fist after smashing a grand slam off Mark Langston in Game 1 of the World Series. After Langston's 2–2 cut fastball sliced through the strike zone and was called a ball, Martinez took advantage of that call and hit the next cutter into the right field upper deck. The slam broke a tie and helped propel the Yankees to a 9–5 win.

A ferocious competitor, **ANDY PETTITTE** pitched seven and one-third scoreless innings to help the Yankees to a 3–0 win in the clinching game of the World Series. Pettitte watched the first two games from his father's hospital room because his dad was recovering from heart surgery. Ready and relieved in Game 4, Pettitte delivered.

Throughout the season, **SCOTT BROSIUS** had envisioned making the play that would produce the last out of the World Series. When that final grounder was hit to Brosius, he smoothly made the play. And then he jumped around the infield as if his spikes were mini trampolines. Brosius batted .471 with two homers and was named the most valuable player of the World Series.

Courtesy of Todd Warshaw/Getty Images.

The incomparable **MARIANO RIVERA** collected the final out of the World Series, raised his arms high in the air, and prepared to hug catcher Joe Girardi. One year after Rivera faltered in the postseason and allowed a pivotal homer to Sandy Alomar Jr., he was almost flawless. Rivera faced 47 batters in the 1998 postseason and allowed no runs and six hits.

Courtesy of the Sporting News via Getty Images.

After the Yankees won their 125th game and secured a World Series title, **DEREK JETER** smiled, put on a championship T-shirt and a championship cap and celebrated. Jeter, the most valuable and the most popular Yankee, said the Yankees focused on beating teams in every inning, not just every game. The strategy worked.

Any time you go through perceived stressful situations, you'd look in the dugout and he was always calm. I can't think of a better manager to have led that group than Mister T."

Sometimes, though, Torre did lose his cool. Sometimes, a player incurred his wrath during a game. Bush called the 1998 Yankees "the gift that keeps on giving" because he wasn't even sure he would make the team. Instead, Bush experienced a memorable rookie season and the season of a lifetime as he hit .380 with six steals in 45 games.

Spending the bulk of his time in the dugout and not on the field, Bush tried to stay alert, ready to contribute. He played in five games in April, five games in May, six games in June, six games in July, and 11 games in August. But, once the Yankees clinched the division on September 9, Bush admitted that "everything got a little stale" for him because, even with the clinching, he still didn't play regularly.

Bush knew his role. He was mostly a pinch-runner, so his job was in his job title. He needed to run and run well. Torre inserted Bush to pinch-run for Chili Davis at first base in the ninth inning of a game against the Orioles on September 20. When Spencer destroyed Jimmy Key's sinker and sent it to deep center field, Bush thought it looked and sounded like a home run and jogged to second. But the ball hit off the top of the green padded fence and missed being a homer by inches. Brady Anderson played the ball off the fence speedily and fired it back to the infield. Bush accelerated and had to hustle to score the run that gave the Yankees a 5–3 lead. Teammates gave Bush fist bumps, but Torre wasn't celebrating and asked him a question.

"What happened?" Torre said.

Bush said, "I thought it was a home run. My bad."

Torre snapped and said, "You didn't think it was a home run because it wasn't a damn home run."

Silently, Bush slinked into a seat in the third base dugout. He knew Torre was right and he knew Torre was upset so he didn't try to say anything else. But Bush was aggravated, too, and angry at himself. His shoulders sagged, his face looked somber, and he was hurting. As the Yankees shook hands on the field after the win, Torre sidled up to Bush, put his arm around Bush's shoulder, and spoke.

"Kid," Torre said, "this is the time I need you."

All at once, Bush was very relieved and very nervous.

"I just thought, 'Holy shit, I got to get my shit together,'" Bush recalled. "Joe was sending me a message about staying focused."

Bush's listless running was a blip on a historic night when Cal Ripken Jr. elected to sit and end his consecutive games streak at a record of 2,632. Still, there was a lesson for Bush: If Ripken could play in 2,632 straight games across 17 seasons, Bush should have been able to sprint for 270 feet in his 50th major league game.

Soon after the Baltimore game, Bush found out that he had made the 25-man postseason roster. As a player who was a pinch-runner extraordinaire, there was no guarantee that Bush was going to be on the roster. What transpired with Torre was another major lesson for Bush.

"Within that hour, the range of emotions that I felt were incredible," Bush said. "I was excited because we won and then

Joe was upset so I was kind of hurt. And then he brought it to a head by telling me, 'Hey, I need you. Don't fall apart on me.' I was like, 'Uh-oh, you'd better get it together.'"

Not surprisingly, Bush has used that story to counsel young players.

"When I talk to players, I tell them that you never know where your career is going to go," Bush said. "You might have to get in there as a pinch-runner and you have to know your value and you have to bring your value every day. Not everyone's career is going to take off like Derek Jeter's so you always have to be ready."

Before Bush's memorable exchange with Torre in September, the Yankees cruised through July and August. One day, Bush heard a statistical comparison that illustrated just how dominant the Yankees had been. From July 26 through August 22, the second place Red Sox won 15 of 24 games. That's a .625 winning percentage and a 101-win pace for an entire season. During that stretch, the Yankees went 22–6 so the Red Sox actually lost four and a half games in the standings. For a team to play as well as Boston did and to *lose* that much ground was depressing and was also indicative of just how overpowering the Yankees were.

A four-game losing streak in late August included three setbacks against the Angels, the only team to have a winning record (6–5) against the Yankees that season. Steinbrenner had a 45-minute meeting in Torre's office before the Yankees broke the streak and, when he emerged, he playfully told reporters, "Yeah, I just fired him." He didn't fire Torre, of course. Torre addressed the losing streak and stressed that he didn't "want anything to spiral" with his team. The Yankees won after the Steinbrenner-Torre meeting, regrouped and clinched a playoff spot two days later, on August 29.

Bush called himself "a utility guy who never played" and wanted to be careful that he wasn't portraying himself to be as important as Jeter or Williams or O'Neill, but he raved about how the Yankees oozed confidence. They weren't just playing a game. They were playing a game they truly expected to win. Reliever Mike Stanton said, "It almost felt like we didn't lose and, if we did lose, it would tick us off and we'd go on another long winning streak." Bush noticed that feeling every day.

"It felt like when we rolled into town, we were definitely going to win," Bush said. "I don't know how to say it without coming off like I was one of the dudes who made it happen, but it was literally a feeling of total dominance. When we rolled into town, even players on the other team wanted autographs from our guys. For real. It was crazy."

The autograph requests from opponents seemed crazy to Bush, but there were a lot of crazy and unexpected things that happened on the deep and talented Yankees. Like a player who barely hit .200 with the A's rebounding to win the World Series MVP for the Yankees. Like that player learning he was traded to New York because his agent sang Sinatra to him. That player was Brosius, who was an unbelievable player on an unbelievable team in New York, New York. Start spreading the news.

CHAPTER 7

The Once and Future
Wonder Boys

On the final Sunday in August, the front page of the *New York Times* was filled with some notable and diverse news stories. President Bill Clinton was preparing for a trip to Moscow to meet with the president of Russia, Boris Yeltsin; more than 6,000 pilots from Northwest Airlines went on strike; and Toms River, New Jersey, beat Kashima, Japan, to win the Little League World Series. And, in some predictable news on the front page of the sports section, the Yankees, those unbeatable Yankees, played another game and won another game.

On a glorious afternoon in the Bronx, a day when Derek Jeter, Paul O'Neill, and Bernie Williams each smacked three hits, the Yankees defeated the Seattle Mariners, 11–6, and also clinched a postseason spot. Yes, they clinched before the calendar had flipped to September. It was the earliest that a team had clinched a playoff spot in the twentieth century.

But the Yankees, so consistent and so ruthless in their winning, didn't even realize it. With 28 games left in the season, no media relations officials had reviewed the contending teams' records and analyzed the potential scenarios. But, about 90 minutes after the victory, reporters deduced that the Yankees had assured themselves of at least a wild card spot. Clinching the division was an inevitability that would soon follow.

Save the bottles of champagne for greater celebrations, right? Three days later, David Wells, who had already pitched a perfect game in May, retired the first 20 batters of the game against the Athletics before surrendering a hit. He would not complete the unthinkable feat of pitching two perfect games in a span of four months. But the beefy strike-thrower had been excellent since that perfecto and, along with Roger Clemens, Pedro Martínez, and David Cone, had been one of the best pitchers in the American League. The Yankees would drink to that.

The next day, Oakland's Gil Heredia achieved what pitchers rarely achieved that season and silenced the Yankees in a 2–0 win. But Heredia had such reverence for the Yankees that he asked a batboy to get him a baseball signed by the team. Even the Yankees' peers were in awe of them. And that was appropriate. On September 4, the Yankees notched their 100th win. Five days later, they beat Tim Wakefield and the Red Sox to clinch the American League East. Their record was an astounding 102–41, even if they were in the midst of losing seven of 11 games.

The final month of the season was supposed to be a tune-up for the Yankees, a way to get themselves ready for the month that mattered: October. The Yankees would ultimately be judged by what they did in October, not by what they did in September or what they had done while rampaging through teams.

Acutely aware of this was Jeter. Jeter recalled saying that he wouldn't have cared if the Yankees finished 150–12 if they also lost the World Series. That kind of season would have been "pointless," he added. As the Yankees peeked ahead to those October games that would define how accomplished they were and how they would be remembered, they suddenly had a visitor.

A blond bomber named Shane Spencer was added to their lineup.

In September, Spencer was the minor league lifer who injected another special and unexpected wrinkle into a superb story about a team chasing history. The 26-year-old invaded the year-round party and forced Manager Joe Torre and the rest of the baseball world to notice him. There wasn't supposed to be any extra playing time on the Yankees. Actually, left field was the team's weakest link and was a spot that had mostly been manned by Chad Curtis, with cameos from Tim Raines, Ricky Ledée, and Darryl Strawberry. The Yankees were competent in left field. So, even near the end of what would be a historic 114-win regular season, the position wasn't necessarily a question mark, until an instant legend showed up.

But the Yankees didn't really invite Spencer to this party. He crashed it and he never left.

"It felt," said Jeter, "like Spence was hitting a home run every day."

Well, he almost was. Spencer blasted 10 homers in 67 at-bats that season, with eight of them coming in September. Spencer's unveiling came slowly as he went 0 for 4 in two April games and logged two more hitless at-bats in June. He pinch-hit for Strawberry on July 28 and notched his first major league hit off Anaheim's Greg Cadaret, but played in only three games that month. Spencer went 5 for 5 and socked two homers in a 14–2 win over the Royals on August 7, a powerful performance that should have piqued the attention of the most skeptical Yankee decision-makers. Right? Ten days later, he was optioned back to Triple-A.

On August 31, the Yankees recalled Spencer from Columbus and soon, very soon, everything about his baseball existence would change. The powerful Yankees were struggling for the first time and were in the middle of a 10–14 stretch so they needed a boost. That boost came from Spencer. Or Roy Hobbs. Or Joe Hardy. Or the second coming of Mickey Mantle.

"Shane was 'The Natural,'" said teammate Dale Sveum. "It was ridiculous what he did with the homers and the grand slams and helping us in the playoffs."

Spencer started innocently enough with a homer against the White Sox on September 4. And then Spencer, who had waited so long to play in the majors, waited some more as he only played a few times over the next two weeks. During that time, there was some Yankee drama. After Toronto's Roger Clemens allowed three runs in the fourth inning and promptly hit Scott Brosius in the back with two outs and the bases empty, Hideki Irabu plunked Shannon Stewart with the first pitch of the fifth inning. Irabu actually ran toward Stewart to confront him and both benches emptied in that September 11 game. Five days later, Torre was so livid about how sluggish the Yankees played in a 7–0 loss to the expansion Tampa Bay Devil Rays that he kept the clubhouse doors closed and lambasted his players. Torre said the Yankees "stunk" and reminded them how their superior play had made the opposition fear them all year. Don't spoil that now, Torre said. The Yankees were 11–1 against Tampa Bay that season.

"We played lousy in that game," Torre said. "I remember that meeting distinctly. I told them, 'You spent the whole season making teams afraid to play you and then you show them that you're just ordinary with the way you played tonight.' I looked around the room and Bernie was nodding his head up and down. I almost burst out laughing. Only Bernie could do that to me. He is such a cerebral individual. Bernie was nodding and acted like I was talking about him, which I wasn't. I just wanted to send a message to everyone about playing better."

Spencer kept sending his own messages with his lethal bat. Finally, on September 18, it was Spencer's time again as he entered the game in the sixth inning and hit a grand slam off Baltimore's Jesse Orosco in the ninth. Showing no aversion to coming off the bench, Spencer smacked a pinch-hit double in the ninth off Jimmy Key two days later to knock in a run and help the Yankees to another win.

While playing both ends of a doubleheader on September 22, Spencer went 5 for 7 with two homers against Cleveland. The next day, he went 3 for 4 with another homer. One day later, Spencer smashed a grand slam off Tampa Bay's Wilson Álvarez. And, giving Torre even more to ponder as the Yankees moved toward the postseason, Spencer bashed another grand slam off Tampa Bay's Albie Lopez in the final game of the season. He made major league baseball feel like slow-pitch softball with seven homers, including three grand slams, in a nine-game span.

"How many grand slams did he hit that year?" Jeter asked. "He hit three in a few weeks. I hit one in 20 years."

The home run race between Mark McGwire and Sammy Sosa had dominated the baseball headlines that season, garnering much more attention than the Yankees' pursuit of a mammoth victory total. The home run battle was easy to follow and easy to digest. Did McGwire go deep? Did Sosa match him? Back and forth, the power hitters went. Fans love homers and McGwire and Sosa provided them with big swing after big swing, even if it was later discovered that those accomplishments had been shrouded in steroid use. McGwire eventually admitted to it while suspicions clung to Sosa.

Still, back in 1998, McGwire and Sosa were the home run gods and they were credited with helping increase interest in baseball with their muscular displays. It was portrayed as two sluggers fighting wholesomely and cordially. And how sizzling was Spencer? During his September splurge, a savvy scoreboard operator at Yankee Stadium updated the home run rankings across the major leagues in this way:

McGwire 66

Sosa 66

Spencer 9

Yes, indeed. It felt right. It felt as if Spencer belonged with both of them.

"When you're going through that moment, you're not thinking about it," said Spencer. "Whatever your routine is, you're just going to do it and you're just going to keep going. Especially for a guy like me. I was going to stay on that path for as long as I could."

Another season, another return to the minor leagues. That's what Spencer thought as he journeyed a thousand miles from the Yankees' spring training facility in Tampa to the team's Triple-A affiliate in Columbus, Ohio. For the ninth straight season, Spencer would be starting his season away from the major league club. Too far away.

In spring 1998, Spencer thought it would be different. He had slugged 30 homers at Triple-A one year earlier and had excelled in winter ball in Venezuela after making some mechanical changes to his swing. And Spencer felt he had nothing left to prove in the minors. This was supposed to be the season the Yankees finally noticed him. But it didn't happen.

"I was at a point where I'd been in the minor leagues with the Yankees for so long that I personally thought my opportunity in the major leagues was going to come with someone else," Spencer said. "I really never thought I would be a part of anything with the Yankees."

Before Spencer played a game with Columbus, he received a surprise call from Gary Denbo, the Yankees' minor leaguer hitting coordinator. Denbo told Spencer that Chili Davis, the designated hitter, had injured his right ankle and needed to go on the 15-day disabled list so Spencer was being summoned to the majors. The Yankees told him to pack quickly and join the team in Seattle.

Excited, nervous, and overjoyed, Spencer and Heidi, his girlfriend and the woman he would later marry, dashed to the airport in Columbus to begin the next phase of his career, a phase he didn't think would happen two weeks earlier. There were so many questions swirling around Spencer's mind. Would he make it to Seattle in time for the game? When would he get his first at-bat? And his first hit? What number would he wear? But Spencer's trip came to a screeching halt before he reached the departure gate.

"I had gotten pickpocketed and had my wallet stolen while I was celebrating St. Patrick's Day in Tampa," Spencer said. "So when I got to the airport to go to the big leagues, I didn't have an ID. I still hadn't replaced my driver's license. They weren't going to let me get on the flight."

The baseball dream, that faraway dream that Spencer had chased since he signed for $20,000 as a 28th round pick out of Granite Hills High School in El Cajon, California, in 1990, was within his grasp. It was a five-hour flight away. And he wasn't allowed on the plane. Finally, Heidi, in a bold and ingenuous move, offered a potential solution.

"My girlfriend had a baseball card of mine from the minor leagues and we told them what was going on and they let me on the plane," Spencer said. "Obviously, this was pre-9/11 so they accepted it. They let me go on the plane with a baseball card as my ID."

Once Spencer landed in Seattle, his father, Mike, who worked for United States Customs, greeted him. As thrilled as Spencer had been to share the moment with Heidi and then with his dad, he wasn't expecting to get so emotional when he arrived at the Kingdome.

Everything hit Spencer when he walked into a major league clubhouse for the first time and saw the gray road uniform with NEW YORK stitched across the front and the number 47 on the back. He tried to act cool, but, one by one, he was welcomed by the marquee players who had overlapped with him in the minors. There were hugs from Jorge Posada, Andy Pettitte, Mariano Rivera, and Derek Jeter, tender displays that spoke to their respect for a teammate who had played 990 minor league games at that point. They knew Spencer's long and winding story intimately and each hug was a little tighter than the previous one. Spencer was floored.

"When I got there, Jeter, Posada, Mariano, and Pettitte, all of the guys that knew me and who I had played with, they were happier than I was because they knew what I had gone through," Spencer said. "I spent six years in A-ball or whatever it was. This wasn't your normal call up."

Rare is the player who spends six years in Single-A, a minor league rung that is still three promotions from the major leagues. Either the player gives up on himself or the team gives up on the player. What kept Spencer motivated?

"If people tell you that you can't do this or you can't do that or you're not good at something, you just push yourself a little harder," Spencer said. "You're certainly pissed. But, the way it worked out, it made me a better player. I was super raw. I wasn't even that good of a player in high school. But, at the same time, I was on the New York Yankees. That goes a long way as you're trying to make it, especially at that time. I was in their minor league system and we had some good players so I knew I could play. I just kept waiting for a chance."

The chance came in 1998, but, again, it still unfolded very slowly. The legend of Spencer wasn't really born until the final month of the season, which made it even more remarkable. And even though Spencer had a month to remember, the feelings of being overlooked remained raw. A quarter of a century later, Spencer still wonders if his career's script could have and should have played out differently.

"I will say it out loud: I respect the Yankees as much as anyone could," Spencer said. "But I'm not the biggest Yankee fan ever. Just because of the stuff I had to deal with. But everybody has their own issues. But, when I made it and saw how guys like Jeter, Mariano, Posada, and Pettitte were reacting to me, that was more important to me than how I had felt toward the Yankees."

When I asked Spencer to elaborate on his attitude toward the Yankees, he said it stemmed from "the way it took me to get there." He didn't sound angry. He sounded wistful.

"But, if I look back on it now, now that I've been a coach, I can see how things are done," said Spencer, who worked in the San Diego Padres' minor league system and in the Korean baseball league. "Teams are like, 'OK, we have money invested in these guys and this is the way you're going to coach these guys.' It has impacted the way I coach and teach. It's a learning process."

"But, the Yankees' way of doing things with their players, it wasn't working out for me," he continued. "I would take somebody's job every year and, the next thing you know, they'd move up and I would be stuck down in A-ball. So you see the business side of it. And, as a young man, you get frustrated, and you just want to prove everybody wrong."

Eventually, he did. But the Yankees were disappointed in Spencer's progress. During the 1997 Triple-A All-Star break, Mark Newman, who was the Yankees' minor league director, had a testy conversation with Spencer. It was essentially a "WTH" call before anyone was using "WTH" as an acronym.

"What the hell are you doing down there?" Newman screamed. "You're hitting .202! That's not going to cut it in this organization."

Spencer defended himself.

"Listen, Mark, I'm telling you that I've never hit the ball as well as I'm hitting it," Spencer said. "I can't buy a single. I'm smoking the ball. You guys want me to stay in the middle of the field. That's what I'm doing and I'm lining out to center field every game. I don't know what to do."

Unsure if Newman believed him, Spencer did do something in the second half. He kept hitting more line drives and, finally, those lines drives to center turned into hits. And some of those line drives turned into home runs too. Spencer estimated that he hit over .300 in the second half of the season.

"I was crushing the ball and I did well in the playoffs," Spencer said. "I led the league in just about everything. I just didn't hit for average. And then they called a few people up to the Yankees and they didn't call me up. They told me the reason was because I didn't hit for a high average. We all know that's overrated. It's such a joke they used that as an excuse because that's not the way baseball is played now. So I was pissed. I was hitting cleanup and I'm leading the league in homers and RBIs. What else can I do?"

Spencer's memory of the 1997 season was fairly accurate. He was third in the International League with 30 homers and was also in the top 10 in RBIs with 86. But he hit .241. In early September, the Yankees bypassed Spencer to call up Scott Pose, a speedy outfielder who served as a pinch-runner in the postseason; first baseman/outfielder Iván Cruz; and catcher Mike Figga. With a week left in the regular season, Homer Bush, an infielder, and another baserunning threat, was recalled from Triple-A. Why didn't the Yankees promote Spencer that year?

"It's so long ago now," said Brian Cashman, who was an assistant general manager in 1997. "Listen, I would acknowledge that when you're the New York Yankees and the type of rosters that we were used to producing under George Steinbrenner, we'd be more apt to import a Tim Raines than to check out what a Shane Spencer could do. But I don't recall any of the specific conversations about him."

With his emotions ranging from enraged to exasperated, Spencer decided he needed to make some changes. He needed to work on his hitting style. To help make that happen, Spencer negotiated his own deal with Tigres de Aragua and traveled to Venezuela to play winter baseball. His goal: drive the ball to all fields and show that he could hit for average, not just for power.

After a few days of "being pissed," Spencer did some self-analysis and realized the Yankees might be right. Or maybe he and they were both partially right. Whatever the case, he had to improve to get to the majors, so he worked on hitting the ball to the opposite field and learned how to "control the bat" better. And, when he waited on the ball more and didn't try to hit it out of the ballpark, he gradually became a better hitter. Across 41 games for Aragua, Spencer hit .303 with four homers, nine doubles, a triple, 28 runs, and 17 RBIs.

The story that baseball fans know about Spencer in 1998 is how he burst onto the major league scene and punished the baseball more robustly than any Yankee had all season. But that story, though true, is incomplete. When Spencer reminisces about 1998, it starts with him playing a bunch of games in Venezuela in 1997. It started when he became a more polished hitter.

"As I got older," Spencer said, "it was easier to admit that was the winter I needed."

On Spencer's magic carpet ride of 1998, he actually boarded the Columbus shuttle and was optioned back to Triple-A four times. But, as long as he received consistent at-bats, it didn't matter where Spencer was playing or who was pitching. He kept hitting and said, "Everything just clicked" in a way that it never had. In addition to Spencer's barrage with New York, he hit .322 with a .397 on-base percentage, a .570 slugging percentage, and 18 homers in 87 games at Columbus. The mechanical adjustments worked wondrously and, once he had results, his confidence grew.

"It doesn't happen very often when you feel that way," Spencer said. "I played for 17 years and it doesn't happen where you get in a zone and you almost know what the guy is going to throw."

Spencer's power surge was mind-boggling, but he emphasized how much he benefited from sometimes hitting in front of Scott Brosius and seeing a steady stream of fastballs. When the postseason started, Spencer, an afterthought in August, deserved to get at-bats. And he did.

The spellbinding journey continued as he homered in Game 2 of the American League Division Series against the Rangers and also clubbed a two-run homer in the deciding Game 3. After experiencing the scourge of Spencer, Johnny Oates, the Rangers' manager, delivered a quote of the year when he discussed Spencer's hitting prowess.

"I'll tell you what, he doesn't get cheated," said Oates. "He knows what that piece of wood is made for and it's not for cleaning his shoes. Where has he been all year?"

Believe it or not, the Yankees managed to defeat the Cleveland Indians in the American League Championship Series without a homer from Spencer. He went 1 for 10. Spencer, who grew up about 15 miles outside of San Diego, had a double against the Padres in the only game that he started in the World Series. But that double isn't his career highlight.

Spencer has a favorite moment that he plays over and over in his mind because it makes him feel like a kid again. But, he admitted, most people are shocked when he describes that special moment. It has nothing to do with his homers.

Since Spencer was a diehard Padres' fan, he knew every player and studied every swing. But, naturally, the player he studied the closest was Tony Gwynn. Like everyone in San Diego, Spencer loved the sweet-swinging Gwynn. And that's why Gwynn played a significant role in Spencer's most memorable moment.

"I got to play against the Padres in the World Series and I caught a line drive from Tony Gwynn, who was my idol, in the first inning," Spencer said. "And all I wanted to do was put it in my back pocket. But it was only the second out of the inning so I had to throw it back in. But that line drive to me in Game 3, which is the only game I started, that was the highlight of my career. There's nothing that can top that."

A couple of months later, a deliriously happy Spencer was standing on a golf course in a foursome that included Gwynn. Spencer was friends with Brian Looney, a former major league pitcher, and Looney had been high school teammates with Brad Ausmus, a catcher who had been Gwynn's teammate with the Padres two years earlier. Ausmus invited Gwynn to play and Looney invited Spencer. And then Looney picked Spencer off of cloud nine and watched Spencer tee off with his idol.

Since Spencer was anxious and was in awe of Gwynn, he wasn't sure what to say to him. Should he even talk about the World Series? The gregarious Gwynn, who had 2,928 career hits to Spencer's 25 hits at that point, spoke about the series first.

"Nice to meet you," Gwynn said to Spencer. "You stole Christmas presents from my kids."

Spencer laughed and playfully reminded Gwynn that he had "about 20 years in the big leagues" and was surely managing fine without the World Series championship share of $312,042 per player. By the way, the Padres' share was $204,184. That day, Spencer played 18 holes with a perpetual smile. After bragging about being a Gwynn fan throughout his minor league days, he caught a line drive from Gwynn, he was part of a team that beat Gwynn's Padres, and then he shared a round of golf with Gwynn.

"And it all happened in my first year," Spencer said. "Where do I go from here?"

There were two sides to the August 31 transaction that brought Spencer to the Yankees from Triple-A. Mike Buddie, a reliever, was optioned to Columbus. It was the sixth time Buddie had been optioned back to Columbus that season. With only one day left before teams could expand their 25-man rosters, Buddie thought his spot was safe. He accepted his five other demotions gracefully, but this demotion stung. Why now? Why me?

After Torre told Buddie the disappointing news, Buddie returned to his locker and was in a cranky mood. Buddie wasn't scheduled to leave New York for about five hours, but he packed his bags swiftly. He didn't want to speak to anyone else and he didn't want to see anyone else.

"I just wanted to get the heck out of there and have a pity party," Buddie said.

Walking quickly through the bowels of the stadium and executing his departure plan, Buddie saw a towering figure approaching him. There was only one player on the Yankees who was that tall, that muscular, and that noticeable. It was Darryl Strawberry.

"What's going on?" Strawberry asked.

Buddie said, "They sent me down. I'm going back to damn Columbus."

"That sucks," Strawberry said. But Strawberry added, "Are you in a hurry? Because the team photo is being taken today."

Buddie said, "I'm not in a hurry, but I want to get the hell out of here."

That wasn't the answer Strawberry wanted to hear.

"Well, I'm not telling you what to do," Strawberry said. "But this team is pretty good. And this might be a picture you want to be in. If you want to stick around, I'm happy to go talk to Joe for you."

Within seconds, Buddie realized the wise and kind Strawberry was right. If this was Buddie's only opportunity to be on a team that won a World Series title, he would want some proof that he was on that team, played with those players, and contributed to their success. So Buddie thanked Strawberry, took a deep breath, and marched back into Torre's office and made the Strawberry-inspired request.

"Joe," Buddie said, "would you have any problem with me hanging around to be in the team photo?"

"Absolutely not," Torre said. "Would love to have you in it."

In that team picture, Buddie is standing in the third row, between the amazing Mariano Rivera and the seldom used reliever Joe Borowski, all because of Strawberry's selfless gesture.

"That was all Darryl Strawberry's doing," Buddie said. "Because of what he did, that's the only reason I can go into any mall in the country and see that 1998 Yankees' picture on the wall and I'm in it."

Long after Strawberry's act of kindness, the impact on Buddie remains strong. And Buddie has made it his mission to tell the story as often as possible because he considers it a valuable life lesson. Sometimes, Buddie said, we have a tendency to get "caught up in personal emotions instead of seeing the big picture." Strawberry wasn't immersed in his own personal situation that day. He thought about Buddie, a man he had only know for a short while, and a man who now has the 1998 picture framed and hanging in his basement.

"Darryl thought about me first," Buddie said. "And Darryl probably doesn't even remember that. But he's the reason I'm in that picture."

Strawberry was almost always featured in the baseball picture in the 1980s and 1990s, for some great reasons and for some sobering reasons. Picked first overall by the Mets in the 1980 amateur draft out of Crenshaw High School in Los Angeles, Strawberry debuted with the team in 1983 and, man, we all marveled. The six-foot-six Strawberry had a long and fluid swing, the kind of swing that drew comparisons to the legendary Ted Williams and that made Darryl's at-bats must-see at-bats. Even in batting practice. Other players stopped what they were doing and watched Strawberry take BP because they didn't want to miss the show. He swatted 26 homers while winning the National League's Rookie of the Year award in 1983.

Beginning in 1984, Strawberry made eight straight All-Star

teams, hit between 26 and 39 homers every season, finished in the top six in the MVP voting three times, and was one of the most feared hitters in baseball. In Strawberry and Dwight Gooden, who debuted with the Mets in 1984 and won a Cy Young Award in 1985, the Mets had two of the most electrifying players in the majors. David Cone, who became teammates with both in 1987, raved how he had never seen two more incredible young talents than Strawberry and Gooden. Both players seemed destined for the Hall of Fame until substance abuse issues and other off-the-field troubles derailed their careers.

Strawberry helped the rowdy 1986 Mets to a World Series title over the Red Sox, after Mookie Wilson's grounder slithered through Bill Buckner's legs. He called those Mets "an Animal House" team and explained how much he loved playing with a group that included Gary Carter, Keith Hernandez, Wally Backman, Lenny Dykstra, Ron Darling, and Kevin Mitchell. Like many of those Mets, Strawberry acknowledged that those teams underachieved and should have won more than one title. Losing to the Dodgers, a team that the Mets had dominated all season, in the 1988 National League Championship Series was especially galling.

After the 1990 season, Strawberry signed a five-year, $22.25 million contract with the Dodgers and returned home. The homecoming was essentially a bust. Strawberry hit 28 homers in 1991, but he was plagued by injuries for the next two years and was released by the Dodgers. He played for the San Francisco Giants in 1994, but he later tested positive for cocaine use and was suspended from baseball for 60 days in 1995. There was a chance his career was over.

But a gushing Strawberry said Steinbrenner saved him and helped him resurrect his career. A bond formed between Strawberry and Steinbrenner, which started when Steinbrenner made it his personal mission to sign the former Met to a contract that summer. Strawberry was five months removed from being suspended, but that didn't matter to Steinbrenner. He overruled any advisers and gave Strawberry a new deal and a new chance.

Steinbrenner's decision was criticized by many people, including Lee Brown, the National Drug Policy director, and Tommy Lasorda, Strawberry's former manager with the Dodgers. Brown said Steinbrenner sent "the worst possible message" to children by rewarding Strawberry with a contract. Meanwhile, Lasorda said any player who violated baseball's drug policies should be forbidden from playing and also wondered why Strawberry didn't serve any time in prison for pleading guilty to federal income tax evasion. Naturally, Steinbrenner defended the signing and his decision.

"What do they want?" he asked. "Darryl Strawberry to continue doing it until he's dead? Is that what they want? I don't even know if the guy can play. I haven't seen him play. We haven't scouted him. It really matters what he wants to do and if he turns it around, gets away from it. I'm willing to see if he can change."

Steinbrenner continued: "Maybe I'll be disappointed, but I think that Darryl Strawberry can turn things around and be a great lesson for young people to say that you shouldn't do it. Anyone who hasn't done it can get up there and tell kids that. But someone who has been through the terror and almost paid with his life can really get the point across."

Strawberry was forever thankful that Steinbrenner offered him a lifeline.

"He didn't just sign me," Strawberry said. "He cared about my struggles and he knew they were real and he understood them. And I think, a lot of times, people didn't give him enough credit for understanding people's battles and struggles."

Contrite about his mistakes and relieved to be playing again, Strawberry hit three homers in 32 games for the Yankees in 1995. But Strawberry said he didn't feel truly welcomed until he returned with the Yankees and played for Torre in 1996. Torre praised Strawberry's attitude and stressed how much of a weapon Strawberry was, even when he was simply lurking in the dugout as a potential pinch-hitter. Strawberry had three homers in four games against the Orioles in the 1996 ALCS and won his second World Series ring, one from each New York team. Knee issues limited him to 32 plate appearances in 1997, but the Yankees signed Strawberry again for 1998 and he was sensational.

If the Strawberry experiment had failed, Steinbrenner said in 1995 that he would admit his mistake. But he also said his critics and detractors should admit their mistake if Strawberry flourished. Well, in 1998, Steinbrenner's bet on Strawberry proved to be shrewd as the 36-year-old Strawberry hit 24 homers, drove in 57 runs, and had a .896 OPS. He played a lot more than anticipated because of Chili Davis's injuries. And, like old times, Strawberry did it with pizzazz.

MAY 2—Strawberry bashed a pinch-hit grand slam in the ninth inning against Kansas City's Scott Service to help propel the Yankees to a 12–6 win. The ball traveled 435 feet and reminded everyone of Strawberry's legendary power. It was his seventh homer in his first 67 plate appearances. And he didn't even expect to swing a bat.

While Strawberry was watching the final inning from a clubhouse couch, bench coach Don Zimmer alerted him that he would pinch-hit for Joe Girardi if the Yankees loaded the bases. They did. According to the *Hartford Courant*, Strawberry ambled into the dugout with a cigarette still in his mouth and was casually puffing away as he stood near the bat rack. Strawberry's teammates tweaked him about his pre–at-bat smoking routine, causing him to chuckle as he stood in the on-deck circle.

"That's Darryl," Cone told the *Courant*. "How many times have we seen that? He sits around all game, steps on the field, looks at one pitch, and hits the next one about 10 miles. I've seen him hit first pitches in batting practice 500 feet without a warm-up swing. This was just like old times."

AUGUST 4—Take two. Strawberry does it again. After the Yankees managed one run off Kenny Rogers, their former teammate, in eight innings, Strawberry belted another pinch hit grand slam in the ninth inning. Strawberry destroyed Billy Taylor's slider, rocketing it over the center field fence. It was the first time an American League player ever had two pinch hit grand slams in a season. That slam tied the game and the Yankees zoomed to a 10–5 win, scoring nine runs in the ninth, in a doubleheader sweep. Strawberry also homered in the first game. He had 20 homers, his most since 1991, and the Yankees were a remarkable 80–24.

After that stunning and powerful display, Torre said his

Yankees reminded him of the 1976 Reds, one of the greatest teams of all time. The Big Red Machine was guided by Johnny Bench, Joe Morgan, Pete Rose, and Tony Pérez and swept the Phillies in the playoffs and the Yankees in the World Series. Not only did Torre compare the Yankees to the powerful Reds, he added, "And we have better pitching." The Yankees did. And, of course, they had Strawberry too.

Yes, Strawberry had resurrected his career. And when Strawberry ranks those people who have had the greatest influence on his career, Steinbrenner has a hallowed position.

"George is number one on my list because I'm better today because of him believing in me," Strawberry said. "He was the only person that talked to me about life and having troubles and how everybody has troubles. He said, 'Look at me. They suspended me from baseball.' That was a personal, one-on-one relationship that we had, talking about real life."

Real life. Strawberry has lived a real life, a tough life. And, when you've lived a tough life and your baseball career has been in tatters and you're in the middle of an amazing run with an amazing team, you keep playing. At least that's what Strawberry did in the summer of 1998.

As the days and nights rolled past and the Yankees cruised to wins at a rapid rate, Strawberry was producing. But he didn't feel right. He had stomach pains, he felt fatigued, he was losing weight, and, most alarming of all, he also had blood in his stool. Strawberry knew something was wrong. But he kept playing though the pain for about two months.

"I was a ballplayer so you don't go to the doctor," Strawberry said. "If it's not broken, you don't go to the doctor. You just work through it. And I worked through it. I was drinking Maalox every day because of the stomach cramps."

Near the end of the regular season, Strawberry finally reported his symptoms to the athletic trainers. The trainers and the medical staff were concerned and told Strawberry he needed to be examined and tested immediately. Strawberry nodded.

A compromised Strawberry was on the roster for the Division Series against the Texas Rangers, but he didn't play in the opener and his pain was so excruciating that he told Torre he couldn't play in Game 2. The Yankees won both games. David Wells tossed eight scoreless innings to usher the Yankees to a 2–0 victory in the opener and Andy Pettitte followed with seven one-run innings in a 3–1 win the second game.

Before the Yankees traveled to Arlington, Texas, for Game 3, they announced that Strawberry had a CAT scan and, based on the results, he would remain in New York to undergo a colonoscopy.

"And, little did I know, after I got checked, there it was," Strawberry said. "I had colon cancer."

Cancer. A frightening word for anyone to hear and a word that Strawberry had obviously feared. Doctors at Columbia-Presbyterian Medical Center told Strawberry he had a walnut-size tumor in his colon and would need to have surgery to remove it. According to the doctors, Strawberry's tumor had likely existed for about two years and had developed from a polyp. Following the surgery, Strawberry also needed to undergo chemotherapy.

The Yankees were readying for an off-day workout in Texas

when an emotional Torre told them their friend and team-mate had been diagnosed with colon cancer. The usually bubbly clubhouse turned somber, with players wiping tears from their eyes. This was supposed to be a celebratory time for the Yankees, who were one win away from advancing to the ALCS. But the mood turned dark and gloomy.

I've never witnessed a more subdued postseason workout than the one at The Ballpark at Arlington. The Yankees were sleepwalking through their practice as they were robotically hitting, throwing, and fielding, but, most of all, they were wondering. Wondering about Strawberry's future. The most important game of the season was a day away, but all the Yankees were concerned about was Strawberry.

With glassy eyes and uncertainty in his voice, Cone, who was starting Game 3, was numb. Cone and Strawberry were friends, very close friends, since their time with the Mets, and this haunting news leveled Cone. A few days earlier, Dan Quisenberry, the sidearming closer who had been a pitching and life mentor for Cone in Kansas City, had died of brain cancer. With so much sadness smothering him, Cone needed a shoulder to lean on or to cry on and he found the most comfortable shoulder of all. Ed, Cone's father, happened to be at the workout so Cone sidled up to his father near the front row seats and talked about Strawberry.

"We were all scared for Darryl and worried about Darryl," Cone said. "But the doctors said the prognosis was very good and that's what we tried to focus on. But it wasn't easy. Straw was such a big part of that team and we all felt for him."

Cone mentioned how he planned to write Strawberry's

number 39 on his cap, a wonderful idea and a perfect tribute. But, by game time the next night, the Yankees' clubhouse attendants had made sure that 39 was stitched on the back of all of the team's caps. The Yankees wanted to win for themselves, but now they had another motivation: win for Straw.

In a videotaped get-well card of sorts, the Yankees appeared on ESPN's *SportsCenter* to send positive thoughts to Strawberry. Tim Raines was the team's spokesperson and, with Jeter standing to his left, Chuck Knoblauch standing to his right, and the other Yankees surrounding them, Raines said, "We just want to send a message to Darryl that we're all behind him. We know he's strong enough to get through this and we're behind you."

Before Strawberry underwent surgery the next day, he actually responded. In a 45-second video message that teammates described as upbeat, Strawberry implored the Yankees to finish their series against the Rangers and ended his pep talk with, "Go get 'em tonight, guys. Get 'em."

And the Yankees did. With Cone's focus shifting between sliders, splitters, and his teammate, he pitched five and two-thirds scoreless innings to help steer the Yankees to a 4–0 win and a three-game sweep. During the game, Torre actually thought his players looked tense, so he had a rare in-game meeting in the runway behind the dugout and reinforced that THEY were the team with the 2–0 series lead. The players listened and plowed through a long and soggy night that included a rain delay of three hours and 16 minutes. The Yankees didn't get to finish their victory until almost 2:30 in the morning. As much as the Yankees wanted Strawberry to see their conquest over the Rangers, he was surely sleeping by the time they completed the sweep. But the Yankees had heeded his advice to "go get 'em."

"I really felt Straw had turned his life around and then, bang, that happened," Cone said. "Colon cancer? He was too young for that. The timing of it all and the shock of it all was a lot for us to take. I was overwhelmed by it. I had felt so good about Straw coming to the Yankees and getting another chance. I knew he was a good guy. I knew he had some demons. But he was clutch. He was perfect for us."

Not long after Strawberry was finished with surgery, he remembered being hungry and woozy. His eyes were closed and the room was quiet, except for the beeping of the monitors. He was in his own world, a pensive and silent place. Then Strawberry sensed someone's presence in the room and opened his eyes. Sitting beside him was Steinbrenner.

"He just showed up unannounced," Strawberry said. "The Boss walked in by himself and was right there. He said he wanted me to know he was thinking about me and the team was thinking about me too."

After Steinbrenner reiterated how much the players cared about Strawberry and how hard they were working to honor him in October, the Boss said, "And they're going to win. They're going to win it all."

Strawberry smiled for the first time in a while and said, "I know we are."

CHAPTER 8

Mañana, No Problema

Any time George Steinbrenner visited Yankee Stadium to watch his beloved team, anyone who was anyone in Yankee-land knew the principal owner was traveling to the Bronx. Actually, anyone armed with a walkie-talkie knew about Steinbrenner's arrival. Why? Because as soon as a club official had a visual sighting of Steinbrenner, he would bark, "The eagle has landed!" across the devices. It was a reminder to Yankee employees to stand a little straighter, work a little harder, and be prepared for anything.

When that Steinbrenner message was relayed on the first Sunday in October, it was probably delivered with slightly less urgency. The Yankees were having a casual workout in a drizzly rain as they prepared to play the Cleveland Indians in the American League Championship Series. Steinbrenner was in a good mood because the Yankees had swept the Texas Rangers in the first round and because Darryl Strawberry's surgery to remove a cancerous tumor from his colon had been deemed successful. Several players visited with Strawberry and David Cone gave his teammate a Yankee cap with Strawberry's number 39 embroidered on the back.

Always ready to offer his latest and greatest pep talk, Steinbrenner spoke with Derek Jeter and Tino Martinez behind the batting cage and made both players smile. Joe Torre rested his right arm on Steinbrenner's shoulder, the behavior of a manager who was perpetually calm and confident. With or without Steinbrenner hovering, the mission for the Yankees was clear.

"The thing to do now," said Torre, "is to get back to the World Series."

While Torre didn't specifically say the goal was for the Yankees to win the World Series, that was understood. Torre was merely referring to the next task for the Yankees. After 114 regular season wins, three postseason wins, and mounting conversations about where the Yankees might eventually rank among the best teams in history, Torre intimately understood how demanding every inning was for his squad. And the pressure surrounding the Yankees was about to grow much more intense—all because of Chuck Knoblauch ignoring a loose baseball in Game 2. Suddenly, there was a lot of tension and a lot of doubt, the most the Yankees had experienced all season. By far.

Before Knoblauch's gaffe became the most dissected and most dumbfounding play of the series, the Yankees were focused on the opener and focused on redeeming themselves against the Indians. The Indians won 89 regular season games and tamed the Boston Red Sox in four games to advance to another postseason meeting with the Yankees, whom they had vanquished in the playoffs one year earlier.

Remember how Torre was unsettled enough with the Yankees to call a team meeting before the sixth game of the season in Seattle? Remember how Cone spoke passionately at that meeting and said that players often need to devise reasons to hate their opponents? Well, the Yankees didn't need to concoct reasons to hate the Indians. They really hated them. The sting of losing to Cleveland in 1997 had motivated the Yankees throughout the season and that source of motivation was staring at them from the other dugout. It was a perfect scenario for revenge. The Yankees would have been wise to play Bob Marley's "Redemption Song" over and over.

"Maybe we can do it again," said Cleveland shortstop Omar Vizquel. "I know they've been waiting for another shot at us, and now it's time to go at it."

If there was a player who symbolized the Yankees' disgust for the Indians, it was Jaret Wright, a six-foot-two, 230-pound right-hander who loved to own the inside part of the plate with his fastball. If a batter happened to get clipped with that fastball, so be it. The cocky and confident Wright had defeated the Yankees twice in the 1997 Division Series and never seemed unnerved. That was impressive because, at the time, Wright was 21 years old and had pitched in only 16 regular season games. The Indians thought so highly of Wright that he started Game 7 of the 1997 World Series over veteran Charles Nagy. He left the game with a 2–1 lead in the seventh, but the Indians lost the deciding game to the Marlins in 11 innings. Nagy took the loss in the game.

The fearless Wright had the demeanor of a robust pitcher who was also a ferocious linebacker, which he was in high school. With a fastball that sizzled at 95 miles per hour, a nasty slider, and a changeup, Wright had said he often felt "invincible" against batters. In 1998, he was one of five pitchers who notched two wins against the unparalleled Yankees.

And the pitch the Yankees most remembered from Wright was a spring training fastball that fractured Luis Sojo's hand.

"He tried to hit me in the face," Sojo said. "He never said nothing to me after that. If you're going to hit somebody, don't do that. We all have families. The best way to deal with it is to sweep these guys, win this thing, and get to the World Series."

Sitting in the crowded interview room at Yankee Stadium before the opener of the ALCS, Wright bristled when he was asked about pitching inside. He dismissed the idea that he intentionally plunked Sojo or anyone else.

"I think, for me, inside is part of my game, and I am not trying to hurt anybody or hit anybody," Wright said. "That is just the way I was taught to pitch."

Not everyone agreed with Wright. The typically combative David Wells, who was Wright's counterpart in Game 1, reminded everyone that the Yankees had a long memory about the Wright-Sojo incident.

"You have to pitch inside," Wells said. "I understand that. But you don't have to pitch up and in and headhunt. That is one thing I don't believe in. I don't think it is right because you can really hurt somebody."

Headhunt is a damning word in baseball, a word that is only used when players believe a pitcher is intentionally trying to drill a batter in a precarious place. And that's how some Yankees felt about Wright. But, instead of Wright hurting anyone with his pitches or even stopping anyone with his pitches, the Yankees hurt him with a relentless performance. Wright didn't last one inning.

On a cool 55-degree night in the Bronx, Wright's first pitch to Knoblauch was, predictably, an inside fastball. Knoblauch didn't swing, but he soon singled to right on a 2–2 pitch. Jeter had a two-strike single and Paul O'Neill followed with a two-strike single to give the Yankees a quick 1–0 lead. Wright was blowing on his right hand to get a better feel for the baseball. But he never did. Bernie Williams, who had been 0 for 11 in the postseason, laced a run-scoring single for a 2–0 edge. Wright's slider bounced between Sandy Alomar Jr.'s legs for a wild pitch that scored a third run. Jorge Posada rapped another RBI single to knock Wright out of the game after 36 pitches. Scott Brosius added a run-scoring single off reliever Chad Ogea, making Wright's final line two-thirds of an inning, five earned runs, five hits, one strikeout, one walk, no hit batters, and no batters intimidated.

"Nothing going right for Wright," said Gary Thorne, the play-by-play announcer, during the first inning.

In the dugout, Wright looked shell-shocked. The invincibility and the cockiness was gone, destroyed by the fierce Yankees. Wright put on an Indians' jacket and stared straight ahead, trying to dissect the blur of an inning. One fan in a Yankees sweatshirt held up a sign that said, "Jaret Wrong," which was a perfect description for the night. Meanwhile, Wells held the Indians scoreless until Manny Ramírez homered in the ninth inning and the Yankees rushed to a 7–2 win.

"We hit the ball all over, and we got five," said Knoblauch, recounting the fateful first inning. "That was huge, especially against a pitcher like Wright. We put it to him a little."

Knoblauch was excitable as he described what the Yankees had done against Wright. It was his first year as a Yankee and the pesky leadoff man was on a team that was three wins away from reaching the World Series. With Knoblauch's penchant for seeing lots of pitches and spoiling lots of pitches, he was at the forefront of an unforgiving lineup that exhausted pitchers. Knoblauch compared the Yankees' confidence to "a steamroller building up steam."

However, the steam roller short-circuited during a numbing sequence in Game 2, which featured Knoblauch.

Fast-forward to the top of 12th inning and the score tied, 1–1. With pinch-runner Enrique Wilson on first and no outs, Travis Fryman, who had not had a sacrifice bunt in the last two seasons, neatly pushed a bunt along the first baseline. Tino Martinez hesitated for a split second before charging in for the ball. After Martinez reached the roller, he pivoted to throw it to first, but he encountered a problem.

"Travis Fryman was way inside the line," he said, "and I had nowhere to throw it."

Indeed, Martinez was right. In a very shrewd move, Fryman was dashing along the infield grass, not along the dirt of the baseline, and that inhibited Martinez from having the clearest path to throw the ball to the five-foot-nine Knoblauch.

"I either had to lob it over Fryman's shoulder or fire it over his head," Martinez said. "If I fired it over his head, it was going to go over Knobby's head as well. There was no room to throw it because he was right in front of me. So I tried to lob it over his shoulder because I thought it would be an easy catch for Chuck. And I threw it and it just hit Fryman's back and rolled away."

And then chaos ensued. Once the ball caromed off Fryman and rolled behind first, Knoblauch didn't pursue it. He kept his left foot on the base, blew a bubble with his gum, pointed toward the baseline, and waited for plate umpire Ted Hendry to call interference. As Knoblauch argued and never moved, Wilson was rumbling around the bases to score the go-ahead run in what became a 4–1 win for Cleveland. Shockingly and stubbornly, Knoblauch didn't immediately go after the ball. When Knoblauch finally retrieved the ball, his throw home was too late as Wilson stumbled the last 70 feet and dived in headfirst with the second run.

"Knobby was just standing there pointing at the ball," said Jeff Nelson, who was pitching. "The ball was going up the line and Enrique Wilson scored all the way from first. Everybody was yelling to Knobby, 'Get the ball, get the ball.' It was a crazy play. And, even after winning all those games, you're saying, 'Oh, no, this can't define our season.' What the heck is going on here?"

What the heck was going on? Why didn't Knoblauch go after the ball?

"I really didn't have an idea where the ball was," Knoblauch said. "My intentions weren't to not to chase the ball. You gotta play the play out. Everything just seemed to stop."

Knoblauch was the only player who stopped. As annoyed as Knoblauch was with the umpires for not calling interference on Fryman, Jim Evans, the crew chief, told reporters it didn't matter that Fryman was running on the grass. When the ball hit Fryman, he was in fair territory and Evans said, "He has a right to be in that position." Interestingly, Evans said he thought the umpires made the right call, but he also added, "I thought the call could have gone either way." That's quite a hedge from an umpire on such a crucial play.

Both Torre and Steinbrenner criticized the umpires after the game, but the fans were incensed with Knoblauch. And it didn't take long for them to show their anger as he was heavily booed when he batted in the bottom of the 12th. After the game, Knoblauch refused to concede he had made a mistake and didn't fully explain why he failed to pursue the ball. He vacillated between saying he wouldn't have changed anything about what he did on the play to saying he should have hustled after the baseball.

The undersized Knoblauch was a player who thrived in the major leagues in part because he was smart and gritty, but he displayed neither trait on that infamous play. As headstrong as Knoblauch was that night, he was in a depressing place. In a 2022 interview, he admitted, "That night, after it happened, it was hell." Still, Knoblauch continued to insist that his lack of urgency was because he expected the umpires to rule Fryman out.

"I thought Ted Hendry was going to call it because the runner ran way inside the grass," Knoblauch said. "And then the throw was kind of to the left side of the base and it hit him in the back and I just said, 'He's out. He's running out of the baseline.' He was running on the grass, for chrissakes."

Reliving the play and the anxiety again, Knoblauch's voice rose a bit as he said, "I know I got hell from Little League teams for not going and getting the ball and all that stuff. But I thought Ted Hendry was going to call it. It was so obvious of a play. I mean, I felt terrible that the run scored and all of that."

Martinez also thought Fryman should have been ruled out, but he noted that "I didn't stop the play" and that the Yankees had to keep playing once the ball squirted free. As the play unfolded, Martinez said he felt like it was moving in slow motion. Or, in Knoblauch's case, it was no motion.

"We were all yelling, 'Get the ball, get the ball,'" Martinez said. "It's just one of those plays."

It was more than just one of those plays. It was an egregious mistake to ignore the rolling baseball, the kind of mistake that could alter the series. And, if the Yankees lost the series, it was the kind of mistake that would haunt Knoblauch forever. In the press box, Bill Buckner's name was being invoked and was being typed onto laptops. After Buckner allowed a grounder to sneak between his legs in Game 6 of the 1986 World Series, his mistake became the symbol of the Red Sox losing to the Mets. Fairly or unfairly, Buckner's error is what is most remembered for dooming the Red Sox, not Bob Stanley's wild pitch that delivered the tying run in Game 6 or Boston blowing a three-run lead and losing Game 7. The same would be true for Knoblauch. No one would remember how the Yankees went 1 for 12 with runners in scoring position in the Game 2 loss.

Some of Knoblauch's teammates were surprised at his reaction to the play and for not being more contrite about failing to chase the ball. On the flight from New York to Cleveland,

David Cone said he spoke with Knoblauch about admitting the mistake and moving forward. Cone was the perfect person to give Knoblauch some advice on this bizarre play.

While pitching for the Mets in Atlanta in 1990, there were two runners on base when Cone induced Mark Lemke to tap a ball between first and second. Second baseman Gregg Jefferies converged on the tapper while Cone glided toward first to cover the base. Cone caught Jefferies's throw and tagged the base with his right foot. But Charlie Williams, the first base umpire, ruled that Cone had missed the base and incorrectly called Lemke safe.

As Cone held the baseball and argued with Williams, two runs scored. The Braves won, 7–4. Cone called it "an embarrassing moment that might have cost us a ball game" and added, "For two minutes, I snapped. I was in my own little world." I covered that game for the *New York Times* and bumped into Cone at a bar later that night. He was draining shots and challenging teammates and reporters to match his alcohol consumption. Yes, Cone was drinking away the humiliation of the night. Cone didn't tell Knoblauch to mimic his rowdy behavior, but he did advise him to be more apologetic.

"I remember saying something to him along the lines of 'It doesn't matter who is right or wrong,'" Cone said. "You need to step up in front of the media tomorrow and say you should have gotten the ball. 'It was the wrong call, but it was my job to go and get the ball.' As soon as you do that, the story goes away. The longer you stay in denial, the more that people are going to come after you."

From the corner bars to the subway cars, the criticism of

Mañana, No Problema

Knoblauch was pulsating. It was percolating inside newsrooms too. Knoblauch's inaction had created a spate of memorable headlines with the *New York Post* using "Chuck Brainlauch" and the *New York Daily News* and *Newsday* both opting for "Blauch Head." The more staid *New York Times* wasn't as harsh and went with, "Hands on Hips, the Yankees Give One Away."

One day after Knoblauch's brain cramp, I was outside the visitor's clubhouse at Jacobs Field with other reporters. Most of us wanted to ask Knoblauch about the weird play again. But the Yankees delayed opening the doors and said they wanted to wait until more players arrived. I thought the Yankees were trying to protect Knoblauch because he was already inside and was the player that was of the greatest interest to the assembled media.

Soon after that, Knoblauch actually held an unscheduled press conference. When Knoblauch was asked if he had watched replays of the play and if he had any second thoughts, his answer was much different from what he had said the previous night. In a reply that stretched 101 words, Knoblauch said some version of "I screwed up" four times. He apologized to his teammates, Torre, and the fans.

"I remember having that press conference in Cleveland and apologizing to the team for my blunder," Knoblauch said. "It was humbling for me because it was such a big play in the game. I felt terrible about that. But the press conference was good to get it off my shoulders."

The serious Paul O'Neill turned into a stand-up comic, ever so briefly, as he vowed, "I know one thing. If there's a ball rolling around tomorrow, there will be nine guys chasing after it."

As much relief as Knoblauch felt, the Yankees were in an unusual position because being tied in the series felt odd for a team that had dominated all season. And, if Knoblauch thought his blunder would cease being a distraction because he had apologized, he was wrong. When Knoblauch led off in Game 3 in Cleveland, he received a standing ovation. He seemed puzzled, but the Indians' fans were thanking him for his miscue.

Being puzzled was a theme that night for the Yankees as Bartolo Colon limited them to four hits in Cleveland's 6–1 win. Andy Pettitte was rocked for four homers. Gulp. Very swiftly and very shockingly, the Yankees, a team that was destined for greatness, now trailed two games to one in the best of seven series. The Yankees hadn't been in this tenuous of a position all season long. When someone mentioned the 1–4 start as being another perilous situation the Yankees had overcome, O'Neill disagreed and explained how the Yankees had 157 games left to right themselves after their listless start. Now they had a game or two.

"I wouldn't say we had lost our confidence," Martinez said. "But we were in a position that we definitely didn't want to be in, for sure."

Roaming through the visiting clubhouse after New York's Game 3 loss, I spotted Steinbrenner sitting on one of the tables in the trainer's room. He swung his legs back and forth and back and forth, methodically and mindlessly. He looked like a boy who was on a swing at the playground waiting for his friends to arrive. And they never showed up. Steinbrenner sat on that table for about 10 minutes, mostly staring at the wall in front of him. There wasn't much to say. Or was there?

"We'll see what we're made of," Steinbrenner said, after he finally escaped his self-confinement. "I think we'll be fine."

How concerned were the Yankees? O'Neill and Jeter used the same ominous phrase to describe where the Yankees were.

"Yeah, we're in a dangerous situation," O'Neill said. "I don't want to sit here and lie to you. Tomorrow is a bigger game for us than it is for them."

Jeter added, "Any time you're in the postseason, it's a dangerous situation. You never like to lose. But it's a seven-game series. You have to win four games before you lose four."

The unenviable comparison to Buckner continued floating around Knoblauch, with some teammates whispering about how it would escalate if the Yankees lost the series. Knoblauch was an energetic freshman at Texas A & M when Buckner made his fateful error. He knew that Buckner, a stellar major leaguer who had 2,715 hits in a 22-year career, was dogged by that one play for the rest of his life. While Knoblauch insisted he was confident in the Yankees beating Cleveland, he also admitted there was some apprehension about now being forever branded by one unfortunate play.

"Yeah, I had a little bit of anxiety because I didn't want to be that guy," said Knoblauch, meaning the next Buckner. "But I knew we were going to win, though. That's what you have to believe when you're on the field."

Do you know who believed that when he was on the field? Orlando "El Duque" Hernández. With a distinctive and athletic motion in which his left knee almost touched his chin and an array of different pitches and arm angles, El Duque was entertaining to watch. For the Yankees, there was also something very comfortable about having him pitch the most pressure-filled game of the season.

If there was someone built for this game, it was the pitcher who had been with the Yankees the least amount of time. It was the pitcher who had left Cuba in a fishing boat 10 months earlier. It was the pitcher who sounded like a superhero of sorts when he once said there were no relief pitchers in Cuba and that it was the starting pitcher's job to "win or die." Jeter agreed that El Duque was the right man for the assignment.

"He wasn't afraid of a thing," Jeter said. "And, if you think about it, he was the perfect guy for that game."

In fact, the *Record* of Hackensack reported how Steinbrenner approached El Duque to give him a pep talk about the most critical game of the season. The Boss told El Duque, "If you can't stop them, we're through." The cocksure pitcher waved his hand at the owner and said, "Mañana, no problema." Tomorrow, no problem.

Was Hernández serious? Apparently he was. On the morning of Game 4, Torre was eating breakfast in the bustling hotel restaurant when he noticed a familiar figure cleaning plates and silverware from tables to help out the overtaxed staff. That helper was El Duque, who seemed as carefree as a pitcher could be. Hernández recalled that Torre approached and asked him, "Do you know the importance of tonight's game?"

With a translator's help, El Duque told Torre, "Of course, I know how important it is. But you've already said it. The game is tonight. Right now, it's time for me to be with my Cuban friends and family. I will start thinking about the game two hours before it starts."

That cool attitude and approach continued throughout the day, which happened to be El Duque's birthday. There is no evidence about whether he had 29 or 33 candles on his birthday cake.

"We were very confident going into the series, but, honestly, after we lost Game 3, I was like, 'Oh, shit,'" Posada said. "But, once we got to the ballpark and El Duque was relaxed and he was goofing around he wasn't nervous at all, I thought to myself, 'OK, we have this.'"

El Duque had it. He definitely had it. After O'Neill slugged a homer off Dwight Gooden in the first inning, the night turned into the El Duque show. One year earlier, Liván Hernández, El Duque's half brother, was the MVP in powering the Marlins to a World Series title. And now El Duque was trying to save the Yankees' season.

Since Hernández had not pitched in 15 days, it was important for him to navigate through the first inning and find the feel for his pitches. But a single and a walk put two runners on base for Jim Thome, who had blasted two homers in Game 3. And Thome almost went deep again as he drove Hernández's changeup to right field, but O'Neill caught it in front of the fence for the third out. The Yankees exhaled.

The Yankees were astounded by Hernández, a mystery man who defected from Cuba and who became perhaps the coolest pitcher on the planet. When the Indians put two runners on base in the sixth and had two of their best hitters coming up,

Hernández didn't flinch. El Duque struck out Ramírez on a fastball when Ramírez appeared to be guessing a breaking ball and he whiffed Thome on a 3–2 changeup, the one Cone had implored him to throw. Hernández was nifty and nasty. It was a memorable night as the Yankees prevailed, 2–0.

"You get guys who come over from other countries with a lot of hype and you never really know what you're going to get," Martinez said. "But, when you watched El Duque pitch, it was almost like he had been watching these hitters for a long time. It was like he knew how he wanted to pitch every hitter in every lineup."

It's not hyperbole to say that Hernández rescued the Yankees. Had the Yankees faltered, they would have been one loss away from elimination and the pressure would have been overwhelming. The incessant question would have been: Could the 114-win team flop in the ALCS? With all that had happened to the Yankees, that would have been a crisis unlike any they had faced all season. Instead, El Duque guided the Yankees.

"I had pressure," Hernández said. "But I had no fear."

After the crucial win, Torre, who watched Hernández dazzle people over breakfast in the morning, was even more relieved that El Duque had dazzled the Yankees on the field at night.

"He came to my locker and he personally thanked me and congratulated me for the win," Hernández said. "And I thanked him and I thanked my teammates because we all showed what we were capable of doing in such an important game."

Torre added, "Duque was all business. He showed us that from the first time he pitched for us."

El Duque gave the Yankees much more than one win that tied the series at two games each. In the relieved clubhouse, it was evident that Hernández had also given the Yankees their swagger back. For 48 long and frustrating hours, the Yankees were an uncomfortable bunch who wondered if their magic carpet ride was about to derail. It didn't.

Somewhere in the clubhouse, Knoblauch was smiling and exhaling too. It felt like the Yankees were in command again.

"I just went back to trying to play baseball and just tried to focus on the next game and the next play," Knoblauch said. "That's all I can really say about it. But, yeah, I thought we were going to come back and win after Game 2. I didn't have any doubts about us winning. And we ended up winning."

With Wells taking the baseball again, the Yankees defeated the Indians, 5–3, in Game 5 to grab a three games to two lead in the series. The Yankees scored three runs in the top of the first and the Indians responded with two runs in the bottom of the inning against a fidgety Wells, but Wells steadied himself and pitched into the eighth.

Afterward, Wells was focused on something that happened before the game. As he warmed up in the bullpen, Wells said some Cleveland fans had made ugly and disparaging remarks about his mother, Eugenia Ann. Known as "Attitude Annie," Wells's mother had died of heart disease related to diabetes on January 4, 1997, at the age of 58.

"I can deal with a lot of negative stuff out there, but when it involves my mom or one of my family members, it really bothers me," Wells said. "So, to those idiots out there, this one is for you."

Frazzled during the two-run first, Wells allowed just one more run after that beginning and finished with 11 strikeouts in seven and a third innings. When Torre strode to the mound to remove Wells in the eighth, Wells argued that he had made one bad pitch all night and tried to send his manager back to the dugout. But it didn't work. Wells was lathered in boos as he left the game, which prompted him to remove his cap and twirl it to the fans.

"When you get a bunch of clowns out there talking about your mother and not knowing that my mom passed away, it really bothered me," Wells said. "What got me more was some little kids out there started doing the same thing. I was in awe out there because I couldn't believe that could happen."

The Yankees were in awe for a different reason: Wells had become Mr. Reliable in the rotation. Torre called him "an animal" who "goes after" hitters while Steinbrenner was ecstatic about the left-hander.

"The guy is becoming a leader on this team," Steinbrenner said. "If I would have said that three or four years ago, they would have jailed me."

One more win. The Yankees needed one more win to reach the World Series, which had been their goal since Torre declared in February that they had "unfinished business" in 1998. That unfinished business existed because the Indians had quieted the Yankees in 1997. Now the Yankees had the chance to silence the Indians.

There was also a subplot to the Yankees notching one more

win: the ability for Knoblauch to finally and peacefully relax because he would know his mistake had not cost the Yankees the series.

Before the Yankees played Game 6 at Yankee Stadium, I wrote a column in the *New York Times* in which I implored the fans not to boo Knoblauch. His failure to retrieve the ball in Game 2 was a disastrous play and, after some initial stubbornness, he apologized for the gaffe. With the Yankees needing to play nine sound innings to advance to the World Series, what benefit would the fans gain by berating their leadoff man? None. Fortunately for Knoblauch, the fans agreed and gave him a very warm ovation in the first inning. Two wins had changed everything.

On the mound, Cone was trying to win a game he had called "the defining moment in my career as a Yankee."

After the Yankees rushed to a 6–1 lead, Cone was in a tremendous position to secure that win and help cement his legacy. But he didn't feel right. He felt weary. He didn't have much life on his pitches. He felt like he was crawling to the finish line, but he told himself to keep pushing. That was always Cone's mantra. Before his next start, Cone would need a cortisone shot in his right shoulder.

Anyway, Cone's anxiety worsened in the fifth inning as the Indians loaded the bases for the powerful Thome. When Torre left the dugout to speak with Cone, Cone insisted he felt fine. That was a lie. Cone threw a backdoor slider that he wanted to nick the outside corner, but the ball pulled on him as it left his fingertips and hung. It was the type of pitch that pitchers call a cement mixer, a slider that sits in the middle of the plate and is almost placed on a tee. Thome demolished the pitch, rocketing it into the upper deck for a grand slam. The booming shot sliced New York's lead to 6–5.

The home run was so loud that Cone said it sounded as if a gong had been set up behind the mound. Martinez detected how stunned Cone looked and ambled over from first base and said, "Hey, we're still winning." Somehow, a shaken Cone notched the final two outs.

The resourceful Ramiro Mendoza, who was nicknamed the Witch Doctor, replaced Cone in the sixth inning and retired nine of 10 batters. Mendoza said the Yankees were "so good" that season that, "It felt like we couldn't lose a game." Mariano Rivera followed Mendoza to pitch the ninth inning with a chance for some personal redemption. Three hundred seventy-two days earlier, Rivera was crushed because he allowed a devastating homer to Alomar Jr. to lose that series to the Indians.

With 57,142 fans howling and anticipating the Yankees' 35th American League pennant, Rivera behaved like a man who was standing in the quietest section of the library. He threw cut fastballs quickly, precisely, and effectively, showing the approach that would become vintage Rivera as he asserted himself as the greatest closer of all time and fashioned a Hall of Fame career.

Third baseman Scott Brosius made a terrific diving play on a Wilson grounder down the line for the first out, Rivera whiffed Kenny Lofton for the second out, and Rivera induced Vizquel to squib a ball back to the mound for the final out. Rivera had faced 29 batters in the postseason and allowed only one hit. There was no pain for Rivera against the Indians this time as they didn't even manage a base runner against him during the ALCS. There was only joy, sheer joy, as the normally stoic Rivera pumped his fists and hugged Joe Girardi. The Yankees beat the Indians, 9–5, and were going to the World Series.

"This means a lot to me," Rivera said. "I was trying to get back at these guys for what happened last year. I had the chance, and I did it. We did it."

Several years later, as the legend of Rivera exploded and he developed into the greatest late-inning weapon in baseball, teammates and opponents searched for ways to describe his devastating cutter. I once asked Thome, who had 612 homers and was inducted into the Hall of Fame, about Rivera and his analysis was as succinct and as accurate as any I had ever heard.

"For me, I think he has the single best pitch ever in the game," Thome said. "You're talking about a cutter that does unbelievable things."

Best. Pitch. Ever.

As humble as Rivera was, he was also proud of his accomplishments. Again, Rivera called the cutter "a gift from God," a sizzling fastball that suddenly started cutting late and moving drastically.

"Any time you start cutting the baseball, you're going to lose velocity," Cone said. "If I threw a cutter, I would lose three or four miles off my velocity compared to my four-seam fastball. Mariano didn't lose any of that. It's amazing how he had an unbelievable ability to combine movement with velocity and control. And he just kept throwing the pitch over and over on the inside to lefties. And they knew it was coming and there was still nothing they could do about it."

Sometimes, Rivera would tell Girardi and Posada that there was no need to use any signs because he was obviously going to throw a cutter.

"The whole world knew what I was throwing," Rivera said. "The only thing we had to make sure of was the location. The only thing I didn't do was tell the players verbally, 'Hey, guys, it's coming.' I would say that 99 percent of the time, they knew it was a cutter."

And, as Cone noted, those helpless batters still couldn't do anything against Rivera's cutter. By the way, not only was Rivera a superb closer, he was also prophetic. In May, I interviewed Rivera at a time when the Yankees had a 24–7 record. I asked him to compare the still evolving 1998 Yankees to the memorable 1996 Yankees, who had won a championship. Title be damned. Rivera gave a quick and definitive answer about the superiority of the 1998 club.

"This team is much better," he said. "The quality we have here is better than in 1996. It's amazing. But the reason we won the World Series is because we did all the little things. We're winning because we're hitting, pitching, playing defense, and we're doing the little things. That's the scary part."

Venturing to the clubhouse after the Yankees had overcome the Indians, the one player I was most interested in interviewing was Knoblauch. Redemption stories are the most intriguing stories. And Knoblauch was easy to find because he was in the middle of the celebration. Smiling and wearing a cap that declared the Yankees as the 1998 AL champions, Knoblauch discussed how making a mistake and being vilified had shaped him.

"Just to face things and take it like a man and answer all the questions, although they're tough," he said. "You see what you're made of when you have to bounce back from something like that. That's basically what I learned."

That was Knoblauch in 1998: relieved. This is Knoblauch now: emotional.

"I'm very, very proud to have been part of that team," he said. "It was humbling, for sure, to even look back on it today and know what a great team we had and how much fun it was playing on that team. I'm getting emotional now."

In the middle of his answer, Knoblauch's voice cracked. Although I could only hear him through the phone line, I'm pretty sure a tear or two was welling up.

"That was a great time in my life, a great time," Knoblauch said. "For that to be one of the all-time great teams and to know I was on it, that's something special. We'll never lose that feeling."

So much happened across those six games against Cleveland. The Yankees encountered their most severe challenge of a blissful season and they conquered it. Wells won two games and needed to have thick skin in Cleveland. Wright didn't slay anyone. Thome blasted four homers. Bernie Williams awoke from a slumber and hit .381. Rivera found his own redemption.

But the two most compelling characters in the series were Hernández, a hero, and Knoblauch, a villain for a few days before he rebounded. Knoblauch was 4 for 13 with three runs scored in the final four games of the series. There were nerve-racking moments for the Yankees, but El Duque issued his "no problema" proclamation and, as Knoblauch said, "the rest was history" for a special team.

"We fell down two games to one to Cleveland and that hits you," Posada said. "We had won so many games and now we're down? Did we win all those games for nothing? You do think about that. If El Duque didn't pitch the way that he did in Game 4, no one would talk about this team. There was a lot of pressure then. But, once we won that game, we were able to breathe."

Still breathing, still battling, and still bullying teams, in a gentlemanly fashion. Next stop: the World Series.

CHAPTER 9

Just Keep Winning...
125 Times

Professor Joseph Paul Torre had an October ritual, a routine that his players understood and appreciated. It was a simple yet powerful ritual involving math. Before the Yankees began each postseason, Torre stood in the clubhouse and told his players exactly how many wins they needed to complete their season as World Series champions. Any first-grader could easily recite the number, but it was Torre's way of stressing how close the Yankees were to the promised land.

"Eleven more wins," Torre told the group, before the Yankees played the Texas Rangers in the American League Division Series. And the Yankees won the series in three games.

Then Torre announced "Eight more wins," to his players, before they opposed the Cleveland Indians in the American League Championship Series.

And, once the Yankees eliminated the Indians in six games,

Torre's math and baseball lesson could have been a segment on *Sesame Street*: Today's number is four.

The Yankees needed four more wins over the San Diego Padres to celebrate their 24th World Series title, a number that was tempting and tantalizing and scary and surreal. All it would take is one strong week of baseball for the Yankees to be remembered as one of the best teams of all time. All it would take is one anemic week of baseball for the Yankees to be remembered as an outstanding team that failed to win a championship. Four more wins to history, Torre said.

"What's it going to take to win the World Series?" Torre asked.

The fiery Jorge Posada shouted, "Four more wins!"

Torre followed up by saying, "And how are we going to get there?"

Posada declared, "We're going to grind!"

Grinders. As immensely talented as the Yankees were, they viewed themselves as grinders. In a year where Mark McGwire hit 70 homers and Sammy Sosa hammered 66 and the baseball world was captivated by their mighty swings, Tino Martinez led the Yankees with a modest 28 homers. But the Yankees had 10 players who hit at least 10 homers. They scored 965 runs and allowed 659, a whopping run differential of 309 that was the highest since the 1939 Yankees.

The Yankees were grinders, talented grinders, because they turned at-bats into epic duels. Nothing was simple for opposing pitchers because everyone was a threat. Derek Jeter led the team in hits and runs. Martinez led in homers and runs batted in. Paul O'Neill led in extra base hits and total bases. Bernie

Williams led in average, on-base percentage, and slugging percentage. Chuck Knoblauch led in walks and stolen bases. With each batter, the Yankees kept punching and pestering pitchers.

"We were relentless," said Knoblauch. "It was so much fun."

Martinez was endlessly impressed with how dedicated the Yankees were, saying it was the first time he had been in a clubhouse where he rarely saw teammates lounging on the couch. Everyone was working. O'Neill was taking extra swings in the indoor batting cage. Mariano Rivera was counseling relievers about different hitters. David Cone was talking to Orlando Hernández about his changeup or his curveball. Those two starting pitchers were part of a staff that featured six 10-game winners and led the league with a 3.82 ERA, 22 complete games, and eight shutouts. Everywhere Martinez looked, he spied a group of professionals getting better.

"I liked reading the papers and everybody thought we were a boring team and didn't have any fun," Martinez said. "But we had a lot of fun in the locker room and on the plane rides. They compared us to corporate guys who took our briefcases and went to work. To me, it was more like we put on our construction helmets and our work boots and we went to grind every day."

Grinders. That word definitely applied to the Yankees, although I would amend that to say they were accomplished grinders. From General Manager Brian Cashman's perch, the 1998 Yankees were an anomaly because of their commitment to a team concept. It would be commendable if every player was a team-first player, but that doesn't always happen in sports. Selfishness creeps onto every roster as players want more playing time to improve their statistics, boost their status, and earn a better salary. That's life. It's a human instinct to care more about your own performance than you do about another person's performance. Selflessness is far from automatic.

"They were just so consistently focused and dedicated," Cashman said. "They never wavered. It's nothing like I had ever seen before. Not that other teams weren't uber-spectacular in that category, but nothing like 1998. In '98, that was a 25-person roster that was 110 percent dedicated to one goal, like a rabid dog. And I don't even know if that's the right example to use. That team was tenacious. It was nonstop. You were not going to deny them. They were hungry. They were starved. And they had one singular focus as a unit."

After the Yankees won it all in 1996, Cashman thought the 1997 team lost, in part, because some players weren't as willing to sacrifice for the betterment of the team. The core players like Jeter, O'Neill, and Williams played every day and remained steadfast as team-first players. But Cashman said there was "a lot of infighting, a lot of finger-pointing, and a lot of second-guessing of our manager" over playing time that "tore us apart." The battle for at-bats between third basemen Wade Boggs and Charlie Hayes received the most attention in 1997. Cashman said any selfishness vanished in 1998.

"It's hard getting everybody consistently together because people might have personal problems," Cashman said. "Maybe their performance isn't where they want it to be. But everything lined up for us that year. For the most part, we performed at an exceptional level and a consistent level, in all areas. And whatever the outside forces are that can wreak havoc on a season, when it was time to play ball, it was left outside that clubhouse."

"People were able to completely, collectively, and singularly focus on dominating that opponent on that day," Cashman continued. "And I have not seen that type of atmosphere ever again. And that's not belittling any team we've had since. It's just showing how exceptional that particular team was."

On that exceptional team, there were some exceptional starting pitchers. The man who Torre chose to throw the first pitch of the World Series was David Wells, the chatty, carefree pitcher who often clashed with Torre and typically stifled batters. Wells had a veritable family album of tattoos on his body, a hefty body that didn't look like a typical pitcher's frame. But his size wasn't the story rolling into the 1998 postseason. Wells's brilliant pitching was the story.

"He had some of the best mechanics of any pitcher I've ever seen," said Cone. "Even if he was pitching at 240 pounds or 280 pounds or whatever it was. And he was durable and he threw strikes. He pitched until he was 45."

Even Torre praised Wells by saying, "You sort of had to challenge him, I felt. Like tell him he couldn't pitch at a certain weight and he'd go out and pitch a two-hitter."

In the hours after the Yankees had clinched the ALCS at Yankee Stadium, Wells was one of the last players remaining in the clubhouse. One day earlier, Wells had asked a clubhouse attendant to wash a pair of blue jeans and hang them overnight to dry. The pants had been in Wells's locker for 24 hours, but they were still damp. An incredulous Wells studied the pants as if he was studying a trigonometry question and said, "Do you believe this?"

Do you believe this? That was such an apt question to ask of Wells and about Wells in this memorable season. Wells, who grew up in Ocean Beach, California, which is seven miles from downtown San Diego, predicted on the Howard Stern radio show that the Yankees would win the series in five games.

Wait, he did what? How could Wells make that prediction and possibly motivate the Padres? Wells was just speaking his mind, which he always did. Later, Wells amended his prediction. "I'd rather do it in four," he said.

Any discussion about the Padres started with the phenomenal Tony Gwynn, a wondrous hitter who won eight batting titles and five Gold Gloves in his Hall of Fame career. The Padres had 98 victories in the regular season games and defeated the Astros in the National League Division Series and the Braves in the National League Championship Series. Still, Gwynn, who played college baseball and college basketball at San Diego State, used a National Collegiate Athletic Association hoop tournament analogy in comparing the Yankees and the Padres.

"The Yankees are the number one seed," Gwynn told FOX Sports. "We're like the 48th seed or the 64th seed. We're McNeese State or Appalachian State."

Indeed. The Yankees were playing in their 35th World Series while Gwynn and the Padres were playing in their second. On the workout day before Game 1, Gwynn, who had never been to Yankee Stadium, visited Monument Park. The first monument Gwynn spotted was for George Herman "Babe" Ruth. Maybe it was a telling sign that the Babe, another rotund lefty hitter, was hovering over the proceedings.

On that same day, Wells, the San Diego kid, called the city

"God's country" and said San Diego and New York might as well be two different countries. He spoke about playing Wiffle ball and imagining he was Nate Colbert, Dave Winfield, Randy Johnson, or Willie McCovey. The Padres were Wells's favorite National League team while the Yankees were his favorite American League team. Wells sounded like a fan, a fan who was now trying to beat his hometown team.

To beat the Padres, the Yankees had to conquer Kevin Brown, an elite pitcher who had one of the best sinkers in the majors. Tall, thin, and expressionless, Brown pitched like someone who was guarding the front door of his house from an intrusion. Brown attacked batters with his heavy sinker, but he also threw a four-seam fastball, a curve, a splitter, a cutter, and a changeup. He was San Diego's version of Cone, a creative pitcher who threw a variety of pitches from different arm angles. Hitters referred to Brown's sinker as "a bowling ball sinker" because it was so heavy and so difficult to hit the ball in the air.

An unlikely source did exactly that for the Yankees. After a walk, a Chili Davis single, and another walk filled the bases in the second inning, Brown faced left fielder Ricky Ledée, the number nine hitter. Ledée, a 24-year-old rookie with 42 games of major league experience, had replaced Darryl Strawberry on the ALCS and World Series roster. The Yankees needed a spark as they received almost zero production from their left fielders during the ALCS with Shane Spencer, Chad Curtis, Tim Raines, and Ledée combining to go 1 for 22 and leaving 17 runners on base.

Looking surprisingly calm during the most influential at-bat of his career, Ledée refused to expand the strike zone against Brown. Even after Brown jumped ahead at 1–2, Ledée took the next two pitches to push the count to 3–2. Brown threw a 94 mile-per-hour sinker, but it was up and Ledée lined it into the right field corner. The ball was fair by inches and even kicked up some chalk dust from the white foul line as two runs scored. As Ledée clapped his hands and pumped his fists, Brown shook his head.

"When I was on second, I felt like screaming and just letting it all out," Ledée said. "All the years, all the ups and downs, all the long seasons, all the time I spent in the minors, it was finally worth it."

One inning later, the Padres responded. Greg Vaughn, who had one of the quietest 50-homer seasons in history because of the McGwire and Sosa home run show, was intent on trying to take the outside part of the plate away from Wells. And Vaughn succeeded. When Wells pumped a 93-mile-per-hour fastball on the outside corner, Vaughn slugged it over the right center field fence to tie the score, 2–2. One year earlier, the Yankees had acquired Vaughn in a trade for Kenny Rogers and Mariano Duncan, but the deal was voided when he failed the physical because of a shoulder injury. The almost Yankee now battered the Yankees.

With two outs in the fifth, Quilvio Veras hit a bloop single that seemed harmless enough. But it wasn't harmless because of the batters who followed Veras. After Wells used a slide step to try and keep Veras close to first, he threw a limp 90 mile-per-hour fastball. The masterful Gwynn turned on it and hammered it off the facing of the right field upper deck for a two-run blast. Vaughn golfed Wells's next pitch, a down and in fastball, into the left field seats to push San Diego to a 5–2 lead. It was the 12th time players had hit back-to-back homers in the World Series.

As effective as Brown was while fighting through a sinus infection, the Yankees did their typical job of making the pitcher work. Take pitches. Foul pitches off. Swing at strikes. After Brown allowed a one-out single to Jorge Posada and walked Ledée on four pitches in the seventh inning, Manager Bruce Bochy emerged from the dugout. The weary Brown had thrown 108 pitches across six and a third innings.

In the on-deck circle, Knoblauch turned to Jeter and said, "Is he really going to take Brown out right now?" As startled as Knoblauch was to see Donne Wall replace Brown, Knoblauch had a plan. "I was looking to do one thing," he said, "and that was to drive the ball."

Despite his glaring mistake in Game 2 of the ALCS, the much-maligned Knoblauch knew this was a new series and a new start. Before the at-bat, Joe Buck, the play-by-play announcer, said, "What an opportunity for Chuck Knoblauch to endear himself to these Yankee fans."

It was a prescient comment from Buck because Knoblauch lifted a 2–0 fastball down the left field line and the ball disappeared into the first few rows for a game-tying three-run homer. Knoblauch was almost at first base when the ball sailed over the 318-foot sign and he flipped his bat aside with a "How do you like me now?" flair.

"The first pitch was up and in, the next pitch was over my head, and the third pitch was center cut and I drove it just far enough for a homer," Knoblauch said. "It was definitely a feeling of redemption. One hundred percent."

The Yankees kept attacking. A Jeter single, a wild pitch, an intentional walk, and another walk loaded the bases for Martinez. Martinez was facing left-hander Mark Langston in an at-bat that helped define the series. It had been another disappointing and frustrating postseason for Martinez. Coming into the game, Martinez was 20 for 107 (.187) with one homer and four runs batted in for the Yankees in postseason play, unfathomable statistics for a middle-of-the-order hitter who had knocked in 381 runs in his last three seasons. In the 1996 World Series victory over the Braves, Martinez was 1 for 11 and lost his starting job to Cecil Fielder for Games 3, 4, and 5.

Still, there was a tenacity about Martinez. Martinez kept trying to find the perfect swing. Martinez's tireless approach and pursuit of perfection were born in the backyard of a house on Kathleen Street in Tampa. There was a five-foot chain-link fence in the backyard, so a 13-year-old Martinez took a bucket of baseballs and a batting tee and smacked baseball after baseball against the fence day after day. Eventually, after thousands of sweet swings, Martinez hit a baseball that tore a hole in the fence.

Against Langston, Martinez didn't need to hit a ball through the fence. But over the fence would be nice. On a 2–2 count, Langston threw a cutter that sliced over the outside corner of the plate and looked like a strike. Martinez didn't swing. Plate umpire Richie Garcia didn't raise his fist and called it a ball. Martinez still had some life. Barely. The overhead camera showed that the pitch had caught enough of the plate, but there was the issue of where Carlos Hernández caught the ball. The pitch was knee-high, but Hernández did lift his glove several inches in an attempt to frame the pitch.

"You know, it could have been called a ball or a strike," Martinez said. "I think the hesitation of the glove moving up helped it become a ball and not a strike. It's one of those borderline pitches that could have gone either way, and, fortunately, I got the call."

Once Martinez got the call, his game plan against Langston crystallized. He was expecting another cutter and, with the bases loaded, he knew Langston had to throw it in the strike zone. Martinez was ready and he clobbered it into the right field upper deck for a grand slam. The delirious fans howled and cups of beer flew out of the upper deck as Martinez knocked in as many runs with one swing as he had in his previous 29 postseason games.

"He threw me another cutter," Martinez said. "It was a little three-quarters cutter that he threw later in his career. That one was belt-high and it started on the inner half and it broke right over the middle of the plate. At that point, I knew he had to throw it over the plate and hope for the best. I know he was hoping that he would strike me out or I would pop it up."

Langston, who barked at Garcia over the 2–2 pitch, was shocked it was called a ball. He added, "I thought it was a strike. Unfortunately, I didn't execute the next pitch."

When Martinez reached the dugout, the first player to greet him was Knoblauch. That was symbolic. Ten days earlier, Knoblauch and Martinez were the protagonists in a botched bunt play that doomed the Yankees against the Indians and created the most distress that the team had endured all season. But, on this night, they both drilled homers and were the main reasons the Yankees prevailed, 9–6, in the opener. It was quite a turnaround, but Martinez deflected the attention away from the swing that was honed on Kathleen Street and pushed the focus back on the team.

"That win, in general, meant a lot," Martinez said. "In the World Series and the whole postseason, there are so many momentum swings. To get a win at home in Game 1 of the series was huge."

On that night and the next day and for many days to come, there were debates about that 2–2 pitch. There still are. It looked like a strike, but Garcia didn't see it that way.

During the game, this is what Martinez thought about the pitch.

"Honestly, at the time, I didn't think it was a strike at all," Martinez said. "I thought the ball was low. Langston liked to spin those little cutters that started at the bottom of the zone and stayed there or dipped down a little. If I'd swung at that pitch, I probably would have rolled over it and hit it to second base. I was looking for something that was up so I could hit it into the gaps or the outfield. I didn't step out of the box and I went on to the next pitch."

After the game, this is what Martinez thought about the pitch.

"I kept being asked about it and I looked at the replay," he said. "And I said, 'Man, that was closer than I thought.'" It was way closer than I thought. I didn't realize that when I was hitting because I had my eye level set up so that I could drive the ball and not just roll over it and hit a routine grounder to second."

During the postseason, the clubhouses are closed to reporters before games so pregame access to players is drastically reduced.

Before Game 2, I lurked in the hallways outside the clubhouse to try and intercept Ledée. Ledée had reached base four times in his first World Series game and looked relaxed against the dynamic Brown. I needed to ask him about the greatest baseball night of his life. Smiling when he finally arrived, a bleary-eyed Ledée told me his amazing night had also been a long night.

Returning to his New York hotel by around 3 a.m., Ledée said his phone buzzed 30 times in the next 12 hours. So many family members and friends called Ledée from his hometown of Salinas, Puerto Rico, that he felt as if they were hanging out with him and sharing his dream with him.

Ten months earlier, I sat across from Ledée at a seafood restaurant in Salinas and we talked about baseball and life and more baseball. I was writing a feature story on Ledée, a promising prospect, for the *New York Times* so we spent hours driving around the island. We even went to see a cockfight. I wasn't upset when we learned the event had been canceled.

When the conversation shifted to the 1996 Yankees and how special that team was, Ledée became the interviewer and peppered me with questions about that club and those players. He was in the minor leagues so I had more stories about the 1996 team than he did. Ledée was itching to have his own championship experience.

"All I think about is getting to the Yankees," Ledée said. "Every day, it's what I dream about. Once I get there, I want to stay there. Then I want to get to play in the World Series."

The 1998 season didn't unfold as magically as Ledée would have liked since he collected only 79 at-bats, but the beginning of the World Series made those limited at-bats a footnote.

That thrilled Ledée and he stressed how much it would have pleased his father.

Toñito Ledée, Ricky's father, was a salsa singer and, after a long night of performing, he fell asleep while driving on a dark highway near Manatí. His car drifted into an oncoming lane and smashed into a truck, instantly killing Toñito. He was 35 years old. Ricky was only 12. The accident occurred on May 27, 1986, which was Ledée's last day of classes in the eighth grade. In Ledée's mind, he went to sleep as a bubbly boy and woke up as a forever changed young man.

"He was the one who wanted me to play," Ledée said. "He was a singer and he didn't want me doing that. He pushed me to play baseball. When he died, I couldn't play anymore."

Six months later, Ledée wandered to Manuel Gonzalez Stadium, a place where his father had thrown batting practice to him. Ledée wasn't sure why he was there that day, but it was fortuitous. Efrain Maldonado, a family friend, was the only person at the ballpark. While Ledée was unaware of this, his father had asked Maldonado to work out with Ledée if there was ever a day when he wasn't available. After Ledée heard that, he cried for the first time over his father's death and then he returned to playing baseball.

"If my father wanted it that badly," Ledée said, "I had to do it."

And, now, 12 years later, Ledée was playing on the biggest and brightest stage in baseball. And he was thriving. And so were the Yankees. As Ledée, Williams, and O'Neill waited to take the field before Game 2, O'Neill spit into the pocket of his glove, rubbed the saliva around, and then repeated the routine. This spit take is only relevant because O'Neill's glove came in handy very quickly.

With the deceptive and mysterious Hernández pitching, the Padres put two men on base in the first. Wally Joyner hit a shot off the end of his bat, but the ball carried to deep right field. O'Neill sprinted to the warning track, leaped, jabbed his left foot into The Wiz sign on the padding, and caught the ball at the top of the fence. It wouldn't have been a homer, but it would have probably scored both runners. Instead, O'Neill and his spit-soaked glove prevented that from happening.

The opportunistic Yankees took advantage of Ken Caminiti's throwing error to score three unearned runs against Andy Ashby in the bottom of the first. The Padres were concerned enough about the sloppy inning to have Brian Boehringer, a former Yankee, warming up. The Padres could have had at least a 2–0 lead in the first, but, instead, they trailed 3–0. Bochy called that inning the "difference in the ball game."

After studying videotape of Ashby, a pitcher he had never faced, Ledée hit a two-strike breaking pitch for a single in the second inning to start a three-run rally. In a vintage Yankee at-bat, Williams fouled off four two-strike pitches before socking a two-run homer off Ashby in the third, and Ledée lashed a two-out, run-scoring double to make it 7–0 and bounced Ashby from the game. Ashby needed 68 pitches to collect eight outs. Ledée, who was the biggest afterthought in the lineup, had reached base in his first seven plate appearances on four hits, two walks, and an outfield error.

Ledée's production in the World Series was another vivid reminder of how the 1998 Yankees were built through some shrewd and late selections in the 1990 amateur draft. The Yankees drafted Ledée, Posada, Pettitte, and Spencer between the 16th and 28th rounds that season, which is one of the greatest late-round performances in draft history. All four were crucial to the Yankees winning it all, with Posada and Pettitte producing all season, Spencer soaring in September and Ledée excelling in October.

With Hernández asserting himself in another postseason game, the seven-run lead felt like 17 runs. After the sticky first, Hernández retired 15 of the next 19 Padres and tossed seven one-run innings in a 9–3 win. The Yankees had a two games to none advantage in the best of seven series. And, at that point, a series sweep seemed much more likely than the Padres extending the series to six or seven games.

How ferocious were the Yankee hitters? From Posada's seventh-inning single that started a seven-run rally in Game 1 through the end of Game 2, the Yankees put 32 of their 59 batters on base and hit .438. They were an army of Gwynns, plus another 100 points of batting average, during that lethal stretch.

"It almost seems," Gwynn said, "like they know what's coming."

Jeter explained it simply because it was what the Yankees had done all season.

"We're being patient," Jeter said. "We're running the counts in our favor. If you do that, you can take advantage of their mistakes."

It was a joyous and exciting time for the Yankees. They were two wins away from winning a World Series championship and validating themselves as one of the best teams of all time. But, in the middle of that pleasant scene, the Yankees had an agitated first baseman.

Before Martinez's massive grand slam in Game 1 and his three hits in Game 2, he had barely produced as a Yankee in the postseason. That deep drought created speculation about his future. If Martinez continued to struggle, would Steinbrenner trade him and try to sign free agent Mo Vaughn as a replacement? The question was asked often enough that Martinez reacted angrily to it.

"I try not to really pay attention to it, but it bothered me because it's come out now during the World Series," Martinez said. "Something like that shouldn't come out until the off-season, regardless of what's happening. I have to admit it. It bothered me."

Steinbrenner called the possibility of dealing Martinez and signing Vaughn to play first base "crazy" and accused reporters of "stirring it up." Interestingly, he also added, "But, if that's got him going, OK."

Martinez was a loyal player and he had once told me he wanted the Yankees to consider his $5 million salary a bargain, which it was. Soon after Martinez swatted a grand slam that was momentous and dramatic, he was being asked about a potentially cloudy future and it stung. How could it not sting?

"I love it here," he said, "but I don't want to be anywhere I'm not wanted."

The center fielder and guitarist known as Bernabe Williams was almost always quiet and aloof. That approach worked for Williams. Williams loved to play baseball, but he also loved to avoid the glare of the spotlight. He didn't want or need the attention, even when he was one of the most valuable players on the team.

And, in 1998, Williams was one of the biggest stories on the Yankees because of his tremendous play. Williams hit .339 to win the American League batting title and he also belted 26 homers, knocked in 97 runs, and had a .997 OPS. But, off the field, Williams's future was also a significant subject because he was eligible for free agency at the end of the season. If Williams was distracted about the possibility of leaving an organization that signed him when he was 16 years old, that didn't show in the way he performed during the regular season.

Still, once the calendar turned to October and Williams's career with the Yankees dwindled closer to a potential conclusion, the center fielder became even more distant. Before the World Series began, Williams even admitted that his aloofness made it seem as if he "was not there." Teammates noticed it, reporters noticed it, and Torre noticed it, causing him to have a one-on-one meeting with Williams.

"Once you're here in New York, you have your life dug into a little bit," Williams said. "I've always taken a lot of pride in keeping my private life private. I don't see why it shouldn't stay that way."

When Cashman was asked to balance the excitement of the Yankees competing in the World Series with the difficult reality of trying to re-sign Williams in the future, he said, "It's a tough thing. You know the ugliness of the future is right in front of you."

One year earlier, the Yankees had offered Williams a five-year, $37.5 million deal, but Scott Boras, his agent, wanted seven years and $70 million. The Yankees decided that amount

was too expensive and both sides walked away from the nego-
tiating table. Clearly, Williams, a switch-hitter who blended
into the middle of the lineup seamlessly, had put himself in
a terrific bargaining position with another wonderful season.

As a homegrown Yankee who had fought through growing pains with some disappointing teams, Williams was a
symbol of what can happen when an organization believes
in a young player and is patient with a young player. When
Williams reached the major leagues in 1991, he often looked
lost and overmatched. But Gene Michael, who was the general
manager at the time, studied Williams's speed and power and
envisioned a multitalented center fielder for a championship
contender. He was right.

Still, as splendidly as Williams's career had turned out with
the Yankees, he refused to ruminate about whether that relationship might continue beyond the 1998 season. As the Yankees were chasing a championship, Williams wanted to focus
on the games and not his future.

"I'm going to have a lot of fun out there," Williams said.
"I'm going to go all out."

Although Williams was 1 for 16 in the World Series, he
drilled a vital homer off Ashby in Game 2. Williams was also
8 for 21 (.381) against Cleveland in the ALCS, which was of
monumental importance to him after making the last out of
the 1997 season against the same team. All of Williams's off-
season work had helped him overcome the anguish of 1997
and revel in the triumph of 1998.

But the triumph of a World Series segued into the drama
of being a free agent and possibly leaving the Yankees. As

Williams described it, Boras and Cashman were at an impasse in their negotiations. The Yankees were offering Williams a five-year, $60 million deal while the rival Red Sox had offered the center fielder seven years for about $90 million. Williams wanted to stay with the Yankees so he told Boras he was unhappy with the way discussions were trending.

"Is there anything we can do to change this?" Williams asked Boras.

Boras said, "You can call George personally and plead your case."

"Give me the number," Williams said.

And that's how Williams ended up calling Steinbrenner and explaining why he wanted to remain with the Yankees and why he felt he belonged with the Yankees. As the conversation unfolded, Williams, who admitted that previous negotiations with the Yankees had been "contentious," could sense that he was making progress.

"We were still in an age where George, as an owner, really appreciated a player standing up for himself and cutting out the agent and the general manager and having a frank, personal conversation with him," Williams said. "I think George really enjoyed that part of the game where he was actually being treated as one of the players. I think he valued the fact that I took it upon myself to take it to him personally."

The Yankees had seriously courted Albert Belle as a possible replacement for Williams and Torre even played golf with the surly slugger. That spooked Williams enough to call Steinbrenner. And it worked. Just when it seemed like the Red Sox would steal one of the Yankees' most valuable and beloved players, it became a George and Bernie show. The owner increased New York's offer to seven years and $87.5 million, which was close to Boston's offer and was enough to keep Williams with the Yankees. The money obviously mattered, but Williams's preference was to stay with the Yankees.

"In many ways, I think that it's kind of a miracle that I remained a Yankee all those years," Williams said. "I know that's where I wanted to be. In the back of their minds, I think they wanted that to happen too."

For the first World Series game in San Diego in 14 years, the restless Padres' fans wanted something, anything, to cheer about. They wanted to believe the Padres could beat the Yankees, not just compete with them, and they showed their support in a raucous fashion. There were 64,667 fans at Qualcomm Stadium who were waving white towels that weren't supposed to be a sign of surrender. They were supposed to inspire the Padres to overcome the damn Yankees.

Gwynn, San Diego's favorite son, had addressed the Padres' 2–0 deficit by saying, "This is the time of year miracles happen. Especially if you make them happen." I found it interesting that Gwynn was already summoning the concept of miracles after a mere two games.

The pitching matchup for Game 3 was Cone, another one of the Yankees' big-game pitchers, against Sterling Hitchcock, a former Yankee who had performed like the biggest of big-game pitchers. Hitchcock was 3–0 with a 1.13 ERA in the postseason and he had defeated Houston's Randy Johnson in the NLDS and Greg Maddux and Tom Glavine of the Braves in the NLCS. All three pitchers had won Cy Young Awards. No pitcher had ever beaten four Cy Young Award winners during one postseason. And guess what? Cone was also a Cy Young Award winner so Hitchcock had a chance to make history.

With nagging soreness in his right shoulder, Cone walked into the trainer's room a few days before his most important start of the season and said, "I need some help to get me through the next start." Cone was evaluated and it was determined that his shoulder was inflamed. He received a cortisone shot and the pain subsided. Of course, even if the pain had not dissipated, the resilient Cone would have pitched through the soreness.

For the first five innings of the game, Cone held the Padres without a hit while Hitchcock limited the Yankees to two hits. The Yankees loaded the bases in the sixth, but didn't score. The Padres did score in the bottom of the inning. Gwynn smacked a two-run single and Caminiti had a sacrifice fly as the Padres jumped to a 3–0 lead. In the seventh, the sizzling Scott Brosius homered off a 3–2 fastball from Hitchcock and another run scored on a Caminiti error as the Yankees made it 3–2.

As the eighth inning began, Trevor Hoffman, one of San Diego's best weapons, was lurking in the bullpen. Hoffman, who had saved 53 games in 54 opportunities in the regular season, had not pitched in the series because the Padres never had a lead in the late innings. The Padres were fearful that they would never get to use Hoffman, who had a 0.49 ERA in those 54 games. But, after Randy Myers walked O'Neill to lead off the eighth, everyone knew it was Trevor Time and time for Hoffman to try and notch a six-out save.

When the bullpen door swung open, the ominous sound of a bell was heard tolling. The bell sounded slowly and hauntingly and it tolled again and again and again. This was the opening of AC/DC's "Hell's Bells," which was Hoffman's entrance music and was an instant sign for the fans to get even more boisterous than they already were. If anyone could save the Padres and revive their chances in the series, it was Hoffman.

This was the situation the Padres wanted: their best reliever trying to stifle the imposing Yankees. But Hoffman, who had not pitched in six days, wasn't the same effective pitcher. Hoffman's first fastball to Bernie Williams was 88 miles per hour, which was several miles below his average fastball. Though Hoffman retired Williams, it was on a shot to the right field warning track. The Yankees watched from the dugout and assessed how Hoffman's velocity was down.

Martinez was patient against some inconsistent changeups and worked out a walk, joining O'Neill on the bases and putting two men on for Brosius. Brosius had only faced Hoffman once and had struck out against him in the All-Star Game three months earlier, but he knew Hoffman threw a devastating changeup and a solid fastball. In that inning, Hoffman didn't seem to have a lively fastball or much control of a changeup.

Hoffman induced a swing and a miss on a first-pitch curve, but missed badly with two straight changeups. After Brosius fouled off a fastball, Hoffman stayed away from his changeup and threw another fastball. The pitch was up in the zone and Brosius destroyed it. The ball carried deeper and deeper, causing center fielder Steve Finley to scamper to the fence before he realized he had no play. Brosius's booming shot carried over the 405-foot sign for a three-run homer. He pumped his arms and screamed as he rounded first base, a World Series MVP in the making.

"This is the type of thing that as a kid you dream about," Brosius said. "I've done it in my backyard 100 times."

From Brosius's backyard to a place in history. With homers in two consecutive World Series at-bats, Brosius now sat alongside Babe Ruth, Joe Collins, Yogi Berra, and Reggie Jackson as the only Yankees to ever achieve that feat.

"He had a Reggie Jackson night, one of the great World Series performances in Yankee history," Cone said. "He just crushed the ball."

Brosius's strategy was simple: stay back and then react.

"I was just looking to try to get something to hit because of his changeup, how good his changeup is," Brosius said. "I was trying to do my best not to jump out and spin off the ball. So it was really just thinking, trying to stay up the middle and try to see the pitch the best I could."

If Brosius had jumped out against Hoffman, he would have had all of his weight on his front side and that would have made it harder to stay through the ball and drive it. When a batter's weight is out on his front side too early, all he can really do is come around the ball and that typically results in a weak grounder. There was nothing weak about Brosius's 424-foot homer.

"We wanted to be aggressive," Hoffman said. "I wasn't aggressive enough to the batter before. I just tinkered around, not putting pitches in the zone. The Yankees are patient, and they're not going to swing if it's not over."

The television cameras showed the reaction of the Yankees after Brosius hit the ball. The players leaped out of the dugout and watched and hoped, yelling, "Come on, come on! Get out!" And the ball got out. Brosius had ignored the ominous sounds of those bells, had conquered Hoffman, and had created a Yankee celebration that extended from the dugout to the clubhouse.

"I was up in the clubhouse with ice on my arm," Cone said. "And everybody just jumped through the roof. It was just incredible. It was almost disbelief when the ball went off the bat. That's dead center. Is that going to make it? And he just crushed the ball. There was nothing cheap about that shot."

From Torre's dugout seat, his eyes fluctuated between watching the baseball and watching Brosius. Baseball and Brosius. Baseball and Brosius. Within seconds, Torre was only watching Brosius.

"When that ball went out of the ballpark, I saw Brosius get to first base and I saw both of his arms go up in the air," Torre recalled. "I turned to Don Zimmer and I said, 'That's the cover of *Sports Illustrated*.' It was just so perfect. He lifted his arms up like he was signaling that the field goal was good. I knew it was a cover shot."

The Yankees still needed to win the game and win the series to make that magazine cover shot a reality, but, really, did anyone doubt that would happen? The Yankees hung on for a 5–4 win and took a commanding 3–0 lead in the best of seven series. The Padres were 92–0 when leading after eight innings that season, but they lost the lead in the eighth because of Brosius's magnificent swing.

"Any time it doesn't work out with Trevor on the mound, you're surprised," Bochy said. "It's tough. This game reaches in and grabs your guts out."

By the way, Torre was a prophet and a keen photo editor because Brosius's celebration did appear on the cover of a commemorative edition of *Sports Illustrated*.

The Yankees' rotation for the World Series was Wells, Cone, Hernández, and Andy Pettitte, a rotation that combined to go 66–26 with a 3.65 ERA and a rotation that Cone called "talented, balanced, and hungry." Hideki Irabu, a starter who began the season by going 6–1 with a 1.59 ERA, didn't pitch in the postseason. Still, in July, Cashman wondered if the rotation needed an upgrade because Randy Johnson, a future Hall of Famer with a 100 mile-per-hour fastball and a knee-buckling slider, was on the trade market. And Cashman was interested in shopping.

As a general manager, Cashman has stressed that his job is to work every day to improve the team, even if the team was on a historic pace. That is why Cashman had numerous discussions with Woody Woodward, the Seattle Mariners' GM, about Johnson. Cashman was intrigued by the possibility of adding an electrifying pitcher while also keeping him away from Cleveland, but he was reluctant to trade Irabu, minor league infielder Mike Lowell, and another minor leaguer.

"I had a lot of dialogue with Woody Woodward, but I never felt like we were in a position where we were going to do it," Cashman explained. "Looking back, I can't remember if they said, 'If you do this, he's yours.'"

The Mariners did say that. If the Yankees had agreed to Seattle's request for Irabu, Lowell, and another minor leaguer, the intimidating Johnson could have joined the most intimidating team in baseball. But, as Cashman felt intense pressure to make the right decision, he did extensive research on his own players and on Johnson.

"Our clubhouse was extremely tight and we had a harmony and the chemistry was perfect," Cashman said. "And I definitely had major concerns about disrupting that."

In addition, Cashman had also noticed that Johnson hardly ever pitched against the Yankees at their stadium. In 1997 and 1998, Johnson made three trips to the Bronx with the Mariners and he didn't pitch in any of the games. Cashman was friendly with Lou Piniella, Seattle's manager, and quizzed him about this.

"And I remember asking Lou, 'Why do we always get lucky and he either pitches the last game in Baltimore or the first game in Boston and we miss him in our series?'" Cashman recalled. "And Lou told me, 'Because Randy doesn't like pitching at Yankee Stadium.'"

Armed with the information, the evidence was now overwhelming to Cashman.

"So you already knew you had a guy with a prickly personality who didn't like pitching here," Cashman said. "So all of that factored in. And we had such harmony on our ball club. My default was I didn't want to mess with a good thing."

The Yankees were relieved when Johnson wasn't traded to the Indians, whom they eventually met in the ALCS. The Mariners traded him to the Astros for pitchers Freddy García and John Halama and infielder Carlos Guillén. Johnson was scintillating with a 10–1 record and a 1.28 ERA. When Johnson and the Astros were knocked out of the NLDS by the Padres, I asked Cashman how happy he was that the lefty he had once chased was now done for the season.

"He is one of those players who is extremely dominant," Cashman said. "I won't say I'm happy. But I will admit he's the kind of guy who makes you extremely nervous. Now who makes me nervous? Anyone else who is going to take the ball against us."

None of the Yankees' interest in Johnson mattered as Game 4 loomed with a familiar left-hander on the mound in Pettitte. It had been an exhausting and frightening season for Pettitte, who was a perfectionist in pinstripes. While Pettitte was 16–11 with a 4.24 ERA, his performance was below expectations for a pitcher who had led the American League with a combined 39 wins in 1996 and 1997. And, as much as win totals for starters are viewed differently these days, wins mattered dearly to Pettitte.

When I interviewed Tom Pettitte, Andy's father, before the postseason, he explained how he wasn't going to watch his son pitch and would instead work his 12-hour graveyard shift at the Lubrizol chemical plant in Deer Park, Texas. Tom had coached Andy since Andy was eight years old and he stressed over every cutter his son threw, but he had abstained from watching recent games because he didn't like to hear the criticism. Andy was 3–5 with a 6.14 ERA in August and September.

"It's not fun listening to people beat up on your kid," Tom Pettitte said. "I have always been more critical of Andy than any New York fan or New York media, but he's my kid. I can do that. To hear other people ripping your kid hurts."

Obviously, any father would be sensitive to hearing his son being criticized, especially since he knew the intimate details of the season. When Andy's second son, Jared, was born on May 28, there were complications because the umbilical cord was wrapped around the baby's neck. While Pettitte never mentioned this as an excuse for his inconsistencies, it was a painful period.

"When a nurse is running to the ICU with your grandson because he can't breathe and he's blue from the neck up, and your son is crying and running behind them and you're running behind him, well, a lot of things happened with Andy," Tom said. "I'm not making excuses. It's been frustrating because we haven't been able to figure this out."

Twenty-five years later, Andy was thankful that Jared was now a happy and healthy adult.

"You walk through life and you know that things don't always go exactly as you planned," Andy said. "Jared had some struggles when we had him. He was born with the cord wrapped around his throat so he spent a couple of days in intensive care. But I remember calling Joe Torre about it and he told me, 'Don't even worry about baseball. Take care of your family.'"

Pettitte had a similar conversation with Torre before the World Series because his father had a 90 percent blockage in his main artery and needed to undergo double bypass heart surgery. Tom Pettitte wanted to delay the surgery so he could fly to San Diego to see his son pitch Game 4, but doctors wouldn't allow it. As the Yankees played the first two games in New York, Pettitte was with his father at St. Luke's Hospital in Houston. The man who had taught Andy his famous pickoff move was fighting from a hospital bed and Andy had to be there to fight too.

"For me, that was a tough series," Pettitte said. "My dad had open-heart surgery on the day of Game 1 of the World Series. So I actually watched the first two games on TV. But he made it through the surgery and I was there for that and for the next day and the next day and the recovery and to see him. For him to say to me, 'I'm good. Go pitch,' that was a relief."

Like a ringer being brought in from a secret location, Pettitte flew from Houston to San Diego to start the possible clinching game. Since doctors had told Pettitte his father was going to be fine, Pettitte said he was adept at shifting his focus to baseball because "I had a job to do and I had a lot of people counting on me." He added, "When I get between those lines, I was pretty good at setting things aside and narrowing my focus."

So true. When I watched Pettitte stare in for a sign like he was preparing for his final pitch or watched him berate himself on the mound and call himself "a big dummy" for making a lousy pitch, I realized I was watching one of the most competitive players I had ever covered. Pettitte was extremely hard on himself. As mild-mannered and polite as Pettitte was off the field, he was every bit as competitive as Jeter or O'Neill or Cone. That incredible focus and mental toughness helped make Pettitte a superb pitcher and, as he grappled with his father's health issues, that surely helped him in San Diego.

Trancelike. That's how Pettitte sometimes looked when he was pitching his best. He looked like a pitcher who was so in tune with what he was throwing that he was barely breathing. That's how Pettitte came across against the Padres as he escaped a bases-loaded jam in the second inning and pitched scoreless baseball into the eighth.

"I just remember everything was working and having such a good peace about myself," Pettitte said. "Things were clear for me. I was in a good rhythm. You kind of get to a place where you have a chance to win a World Series and you just hope you can get your stuff going and you hope you can mentally get locked in. The game slows down for you. It's not always easy to get to that place. But it was one of those nights where I was able to do that."

In what could have been Williams's penultimate at-bat as a Yankee, his bases-loaded chopper to Brown delivered the first run in the sixth. Brosius—who else?—blooped a single over a drawn-in infield to knock in another run and Ledée—also, who else?—had a sacrifice fly to give the Yankees a 3–0 edge. That was the final score as the Yankees swept the series in four games. Ledée went 6 for 10 (.600 average) with four RBIs in the series. How meaningful was that performance to Ledée? One of his future email addresses included a part of his name followed by the number 600.

After the series ended, this is what the Padres lamented: They had a three-run lead in the seventh inning of Game 1, a three-run lead in the seventh inning of Game 3, and they were tied through five innings of Game 4. And the Padres lost every game while being swept. What happened? Well, basically, the Yankees happened. The bigger the situation was and the later the situation was, the better the Yankees were.

"We just ran into a team that's going to go down as one of the best of all time," Bochy said.

Pitch after nasty pitch, Pettitte remained focused because he knew his father was in a safe place. But Pettitte wasn't the only Yankee who was thinking about his father. Maury Brosius had been battling colon cancer so Scott, his highly productive son, was excited that his dad attended the games in San Diego and had a blessing of a distraction through baseball. Meanwhile, Knoblauch's father, Ray, who had advanced-stage Alzheimer's disease, was also at Games 3 and 4. Ray, a former minor league pitcher, was Chuck's high school coach and his forever coach. When Chuck was interested in pitching, Ray built him a mound in the backyard. The father and son bonded over baseball so Chuck was comforted by his dad's presence in San Diego.

"As my mom put it, he didn't know where he was," Knoblauch said. "But I was thrilled that he was there, as I knew his days were limited. I'm glad they were there to experience winning a World Series with them. It was amazing on one hand and very sad on the other. It was nice to experience winning and him being there was special."

Strawberry wasn't in San Diego, but he remained a special

and significant part of the Yankees and their title run. The Yankees wore Strawberry's number 39 on their caps throughout the postseason and the players consistently visited with their recovering teammate. Minutes after the Yankees clinched, Wells summoned his teammates to a corner of the clubhouse, lifted a bottle of champagne and screamed, "This is for the Straw Man!"

The Padres' last gasp occurred as they loaded the bases with two outs in the eighth inning for Jim Leyritz, who had four homers in the postseason and who had also hit two of the most memorable homers in recent Yankees postseason history. Leyritz was nicknamed "The King" because of his brash attitude and his steadfast belief in himself. He had caught Rivera, but did that knowledge even matter? Hardly. Rivera retired Leyritz on a knuckling line drive to center field for the third out. Pettitte, who was clutching a white towel in the dugout, exhaled.

Rivera collected a double play for the first two outs in the ninth and then faced pinch-hitter Mark Sweeney. And, suddenly, the baseball was bounding toward Brosius. It was about to be the final out of the World Series, a once-in-a-lifetime opportunity for Brosius. But Brosius felt as if this had happened before.

Every time Willie Randolph, the third base coach and a former All-Star second baseman, would work with the infielders, Brosius had an interesting routine. For the last grounder that Randolph smacked to him, Brosius would act as if he was making the final play of the World Series. And Brosius took this routine very, very seriously.

"When I came over to this team, my whole thought at the time was, 'OK, my last ground ball every day was two outs in the World Series,'" Brosius told Sweeny Murti of WFAN radio. "I mean, literally, I would say it out loud. I would go, 'Let's go! Two outs! Last out of the World Series!'"

Serendipitously, the play Brosius had envisioned dozens of times actually happened. He took one step back to position himself to field Sweeney's one-hopper, he used a four-seam grip on the baseball, and he fired it across the diamond. Could this play finally be real?

"And, so, when that ball came to me, it was almost like, 'No way,'" Brosius told Murti. "And so I made the throw and I looked back later and didn't even know it, but I'm kind of jumping around. I joked that half of it was I was so excited that I didn't airmail it and throw it 10 rows into the stands because I was so pumped about the last ball and getting that last out."

Fittingly, Brosius, who was the MVP of the World Series after hitting .471 with two homers and six RBIs, was responsible for the final out of the final game. Fittingly, the Yankees, who had been the best team all season, earned their 125th win and won a title. Fittingly, the Yankees celebrated a spectacular season, a season that was as remarkable as any in their illustrious history. Professor Torre's team had finished the math assignment and the baseball assignment. There were no more wins to chase.

CHAPTER 10

Simply the Best

The visiting clubhouse in San Diego was too soggy, too sweaty, and too sticky as the 1998 Yankees swept the Padres in four games and joyously celebrated winning their 24th World Series title. The players raised bottles of Perrier-Jouët champagne and sprayed the bubbly here, there, and everywhere. They chanted Darryl Strawberry's name and Scott Brosius's name and reveled in a baseball season that might have been more dominant than any other.

I was part of that unforgettable scene as a reporter, navigating around the cramped clubhouse with the sheets of plastic covering the lockers to continually ask the same, pertinent question: After winning an unprecedented 125 games and pummeling teams along the way, were these Yankees, the Yankees of Jeter and Mariano, Bernie and O'Neill, Tino and Brosius, and Cone and Wells, the best team ever?

It was a weighty question, a question that was difficult to answer conclusively then and is still challenging to answer now. Babe Ruth and Lou Gehrig are two of the greatest and most renowned players of all time and they combined to hit 107 homers for the 1927 Yankees. Good luck beating them. Joe DiMaggio hit .381 and won the MVP for the 1939 Yankees, who outscored the opposition by a record-setting 411 runs. Have fun trying to defeat them. Roger Maris and Mickey Mantle had an epic home run duel for the 1961 Yankees. Try topping the M&M Boys. The 1976 Cincinnati Reds really were a Big Red Machine and had a lineup flooded with iconic players, from Pete Rose to Joe Morgan to Johnny Bench to Tony Pérez. They were relentless. Connie Mack's 1929 Athletics were guided by Hall of Famers Jimmie Foxx and Lefty Grove. Those teams deserve to be prominently mentioned in any discussion about the best team ever. The 1906 Cubs, the 1942 St. Louis Cardinals, the 1909 Pirates, the 1970 Orioles, the 1986 Mets, the 2018 Red Sox, and perhaps your favorite team should be acknowledged too. But, as the 1998 Yankees maneuvered through their special season and eventually won a title, it was appropriate to wonder how high they deserve to be ranked in history.

Of course, George Steinbrenner, the always demanding and always opinionated owner, stood in that clubhouse in San Diego and instantly assessed where the Yankees should be ranked. Through teary eyes, which was probably 90 percent emotional and 10 percent the sting of the champagne, Steinbrenner classified those Yankees as the greatest.

"Right now, you would have to call them the best team ever," Steinbrenner said. "Based on the record, that's what they are."

He was right. No team had ever accomplished what the Yankees had done in winning 125 games. But was Steinbrenner right in saying the 1998 Yankees should be called the best team ever? I think he was right to feel that way and I will explain why.

There's no foolproof way to evaluate one team against another because there are so many things that have changed across almost 150 years of baseball. Every era is different and features some changes. Every era is better than the last era because, through evolution, we understand that players get bigger and stronger, and faster. Your favorite players are typically better than your grandfather's favorite players.

From the earliest days of baseball until now, there have been massive changes in the sport. There have been dramatic changes in technology with players now using iPads in the dugout and teams using high-speed cameras to assess their pitches and their swings. There have been significant changes in the way that players train, in the way they eat and drink, in the equipment they use, and in the pervasive coaching they receive. Bullpen specialization has forever changed the sport, with batters facing three or four different pitchers in a game. The substantial increase in shifts changed the way teams defended against hitters. Extreme shifts were banned before the 2023 season. There have been expansions in the number of teams, in how much those teams travel, and in the way they travel. The media scrutiny and fan expectations have also intensified. On and on, today's game is different than yesterday's game, last year's game, and the last era's game, making head-to-head comparisons a tricky proposition.

One seismic, welcome, and embarrassingly overdue change occurred when Jackie Robinson broke the color barrier with the Brooklyn Dodgers in 1947. Before then, Black players weren't permitted to play in the major leagues. So there are many historic teams who never played a big-league game against a person of color. If the best players weren't allowed to play, how could a team before 1947 be called one of the best teams ever? As tremendous as those pre-segregation teams were against the competition they faced, they weren't facing the best players. Can they still be the best team ever? I say no. At the very least, the 1998 Yankees are the greatest team in the history of integrated baseball, but I think they're more than that. I think they're the best of all time.

It's important to define my criteria for selecting the greatest team. While some teams have had dynastic runs in winning multiple titles, like the 1936–1939 Yankees, the 1949–1953 Yankees, the 1972–1974 Oakland A's, the 1975–1976 Cincinnati Reds, and the 1998–2000 Yankees, picking the best team of all time, for our purposes here, is about one season.

This isn't about who had the most Hall of Fame players or the most perennial All-Stars. This is about what a team did in that specific season. And, obviously, if the team had players who became Hall of Famers, they surely contributed in a vital way in that one season. But, when we're talking about the finest team ever, we need to analyze that one season and not an entire career or an entire dynasty.

"Greatness, to me, means dominance," said John Thorn, who has been Major League Baseball's official historian since 2011.

Dominance. That's the word that needs to follow the best team of all time and the 1998 Yankees were dominant. Again, no other team has ever won 125 games and, while that total is partially a product of the three-round playoff system (that included the possibility of four rounds for some teams starting in 2022), the three-round format had been in place since 1995. Since then, there have been dozens of playoff teams and none have come close to 125 victories. For the regular season and postseason, the Yankees had a .714 winning percentage, which is the fourth-best of all time, trailing the 1906 Cubs (.747, 118–60), the 1927 Yankees (.722, 114–44), and the 1909 Pirates (.717, 114–45).

In evaluating a team for overall dominance, the 1998 Yankees were supreme in every category. You want offense? The Yankees averaged 5.96 runs per game to lead the majors. You want pitching? The Yankees allowed 4.05 runs per game, which led the American League. You want defense? The Yankees ranked first in the majors in defensive efficiency, according to baseball-reference.com, and had the fourth-fewest errors in baseball. You want dominance? The Yankees outscored their opponents by 309 runs, a run differential that was the highest since the 1939 Yankees. Why does run differential matter? Great teams often overwhelm teams with blowout wins and aren't as reliant on squeaking out wins in one-run games. They're dominating the opposition.

"From the first man to the 25th man on the roster, I don't think there's a team that had more talent and a team whose players knew their roles as well as our players did," said pitcher David Cone. "If you're using that as a barometer for the best team of all time, then I think you can call us the best team of all time."

Always cagey and savvy, Cone's response about the roster and the roles is illuminating because it speaks to how deep and versatile the '98 Yankees were. Sure, the Yankees didn't have two players who could come close to approximating what Ruth (.356, 60 homers, 165 RBIs, 1.258 OPS) and Gehrig (.373, 47 homers, 175 RBIs, 1.240 OPS) did. No team ever has. But, as Cone said, the Yankees had a slew of players who capably filled roles, big and small. Those roles range from Bernie Williams hitting cleanup and winning a batting title with a .339 average to Homer Bush being mostly known as a pinch-runner while also hitting .380 across 45 games.

The '98 Yankees had nine starters who all had an on-base percentage (OBP) of .350 or better, they had a group of over-qualified reserves who actually had a higher OBP than the starters, they had a lead in 48 straight games, they didn't lose in 24 straight series, they went 120–1 when they had the lead after eight innings, they won nine games in which they battered the opponents by at least 10 runs, and more than one-third of their victories came by five runs or more. All of this adds up to dominance.

"When we went into other ballparks, we had so much confidence that it was almost like we were mocking them," said pitcher David Wells. "But we weren't doing that. We weren't rubbing it in their face. We were just saying, 'You know what? We're coming in here with swagger and we're not trying to show you up. But we're going to kick the crap out of you.' And then we'd go to the next city. That was our mindset."

That mindset permeated the postseason as well. The 1998 Yankees needed to win three rounds of playoffs to solidify their status as one of the greatest teams of all-time, something the 1927 Yankees, the 1939 Yankees and dozens of other contending teams didn't have to do. Before the playoffs expanded for the first time in 1969, teams had to win one best of seven series to secure a World Series title.

As powerful and talented as a team might be, the more series that a club has to win in the postseason, the more likely it is to eventually lose one of those series. Even elite teams can lose a short series. Across the last decade, the Los Angeles Dodgers have been the premier team in the major leagues and they have managed to win one championship and that happened in a truncated 60-game regular season in 2020. That is simply a recent reminder of how hard it is to win series after series.

But, while playing against the best competition and during the most intense time of the season, the 1998 Yankees won 11 of 13 games in October and outscored the opposition, 62-34. The Yankees had three postseason series and swept two of them. When the Yankees peeked at their looming mortality before Game 4 of the ALCS in Cleveland, they stared at that possible calamity and unleashed a seven-game winning streak in which they pounded opponents, 44-21. They were a dominant team who finished the season with utter dominance.

Talking baseball with Thorn, an engaging sports historian and author, is a treat. He is knowledgeable enough to cite the exploits of the 1876 Chicago White Stockings as if he was discussing a team he watched last night and pithy enough to say that most examples of teams having great chemistry are bogus. At 76 years old, Thorn has enjoyed a love affair with baseball since he was a boy. Thorn's family emigrated from a Displaced Persons camp in occupied Germany to the Bronx when he was two years old. Eventually, young John noticed that the neighborhood kids cared deeply about baseball. He quickly realized it was something he should care deeply about too. Naturally, MLB's official historian was the perfect person to delve into baseball's deep history and pick the greatest team ever.

"I've got to rank the 1998 Yankees as tops," Thorn said.

When I asked Thorn why that Yankee team resonated with him, he noted how Scott Brosius and Shane Spencer had the "peak seasons" of their careers and how a still young Jeter had a superb offensive season and was also steady defensively. Thorn praised the middle of the Yankees' order as being formidable, with Williams notching a .997 OPS and Tino Martinez and Paul O'Neill combining for 52 homers and 239 RBIs. Delving deeper, Thorn felt Chuck Knoblauch, a first-year Yankee, was a feisty player at the top of the lineup, that switch-hitter Jorge Posada proved he was a stellar catcher, and that Darryl Strawberry revived his career with 24 homers in only 298 at-bats.

On their pitching staff, the Yankees had three aces in Cone, Wells, and Andy Pettitte and a pitcher who performed like an ace in Orlando "El Duque" Hernández. Hideki Irabu even contributed 13 wins as the rotation had a 79–35 record. The bullpen was anchored by Mariano Rivera, the almost infallible closer who had a 1.91 ERA, saved 36 games, and wasn't haunted by Sandy Alomar Jr.'s homer in the '97 playoffs. Mike

Stanton and Jeff Nelson were solid set-up men and Graeme Lloyd was a left-handed specialist who held batters to a .191 average. Ramiro Mendoza was such a multipurpose weapon, moving between the rotation and the bullpen, that he pitched a shutout and also saved a game. The staff was 11–2 with a 2.42 ERA in the postseason.

"So where did they not dominate?" Thorn said. "You could have played that Yankees team against the American League All-Stars in a seven-game series and the Yankees would have won."

That's quite a compliment. The Yankees didn't have any superstars on their 1998 team. Yet, both Jeter and Rivera were on the verge of superstardom and would become first ballot Hall of Famers. Williams, Jorge Posada, Pettitte, and Cone all fashioned careers that garnered them some Hall of Fame votes. But, again, this isn't about the Hall. This is about one season in time. O'Neill and Martinez, both intense as anyone in the dugout, delivered the intensity and the production that the Yankees expected.

But what was also crucial in distinguishing the 1998 team was something Thorn referenced: the surprise seasons. When teams have extraordinary seasons, there are often players who did more than was anticipated. For the Yankees, there were three players who overachieved and were godsends in Brosius, Hernández, and Spencer. Not even the most optimistic Yankee officials could have envisioned their memorable and splashy seasons. Brosius was the World Series MVP, Hernández didn't blink and won the most pressure-filled game of the year in the American League Championship Series, and

Spencer was their most prodigious hitter in September and also clubbed two homers in October.

"Without those three," Cone said, "we don't end up where we did."

Beyond those valuable contributions, the Yankees also had the type of bench players who were overqualified for their roles. Tim Raines, another future Hall of Famer at the end of his career, was a part-time player. Strawberry, a magnetic name in New York and a man who hit 335 career homers, was so chill about his at-bats that he actually implored Joe Torre to start others ahead of him. While injuries limited Chili Davis to 35 games, a player who finished with 350 homers in his career was a valuable asset on the roster. Sometimes, players with glossy résumés, even if they're older, don't want to be relegated to a lesser role. But Strawberry said "there were no egos" on the team and no animosity about who played. Even Thorn noticed that and grudgingly cited their chemistry.

"I hate to talk about intangibles like camaraderie and team spirit because it's largely bullshit," Thorn said. "But I have the feeling that there was something going on with the Yankees, that they had an esprit de corps and that they knew they were good."

After describing the 1998 New York Yankees as kings of the hill and top of the heap, Thorn also said it was appropriate and important to acknowledge some other historic teams, including the 1927 Yankees, the 1976 Reds, the 1929 A's, the 1939 Yankees, and the 1906 Cubs.

The 1927 Yankees—Ruth and Gehrig were the most lethal 3–4 hitters in history and they were the behemoths in a "Murderers' Row" lineup that powered the team to a 110–44 record. The numbers from that squad are numbing. The Yankees outscored opponents by a whopping 376 runs, the second-highest run differential since 1900, and they also led the majors in runs scored (6.3) and runs allowed (3.9) per game, one of only five teams since 1900 to finish first in both categories. The intimidating Ruth had a .772 slugging percentage, a touch higher than Gehrig's .765. Center fielder Earle Combs hit .356, left fielder Bob Meusel hit .337 with 103 RBIs, and second baseman Tony Lazzeri hit .309 and knocked in 102 runs.

When your team is dubbed "Murderers' Row," the pitchers don't get a lot of acclaim, but the Yankees had a very strong staff. Led by Waite Hoyt (22–7, 2.63 ERA), the pitchers had a 3.20 ERA, which also led the majors. Many baseball historians believe the 1927 Yankees, those larger-than-life titans, were the best team of all time.

"When you talk about the 1927 Yankees and you look at that lineup, you're probably like, 'Man, how can we compare to that?'" Posada said. "But our record shows we did. And you're talking about the studs they had and the great home run hitters they had. It's just crazy, but we belonged. Our team was special. It really was about a brotherhood and it was a family. And the way we played in 1998? It's just crazy to think about what we did."

The 1976 Reds—The Reds led the majors in runs per game, batting average, on-base percentage, and slugging percentage. Five of their starters hit over .300, with Joe Morgan, the MVP in 1975 and 1976, slugging 27 homers, driving in 111 runs, and accumulating an OPS of 1.020. As overpowering as the Reds' offense was, they ranked 11th in the majors in runs allowed per game and their pitching staff was league average, suggesting that the team was really carried by a historic offense. In the postseason, the Reds defeated the Phillies in three games in the National League Championship Series and then swept the Yankees in four games in the World Series.

Morgan, the Hall of Fame second baseman who flapped his left elbow before every pitch while hitting, was a broadcaster in 1998. Naturally, he was very proud of what the Reds had accomplished and said center fielder Bernie Williams was the only player from the 1998 Yankees who would have started on the 1976 Reds. I think he was wrong, but I don't blame Morgan for feeling that passionately about his team.

"I really like watching this team, but I'm not going to lie to you and say I think they're better than the one I played for," Morgan told Gannett News Service. "Because I don't think they are."

The 1939 Yankees—Call them the rulers of run differential. The 1939 Yankees outscored opponents by a record 411 runs in steamrolling to a 106–45 record. When they swept the Reds in the World Series, it was their fourth straight title. But, of the four, this team was the best of the bunch. With an MLB best 6.36 runs scored per game and an MLB best 3.66 runs allowed per game, the Yankees outscored opponents by 2.7 runs per game. DiMaggio ripped 30 homers, had 126 RBIs, and had a .671 slugging percentage to win the MVP while four other regulars hit over .300. The pitching staff was led by Hall of Famers Red Ruffing and Lefty Gomez.

Since Gehrig only played eight games and was forced to retire because of his battle with ALS, the 1939 team's outstanding performance was somewhat surprising to Thorn. Babe Dahlgren replaced Gehrig at first and batted .235 with 15 homers and 89 RBIs, which was far inferior to Gehrig's typical statistics. But the Yankees still soared and swept the Reds in the World Series.

The 1929 A's—Connie Mack managed the A's from 1901 to 1950 and, across that half century, this was his finest team. And it was a superb team. The A's went 104–46 and had a run differential of 286, which is the 12th best since 1900. Lefty Grove was Mack's ace and he went 20–6 with a 2.81 ERA to front a staff that allowed the fewest runs in the majors, more than half a run better than any other team. If there was something to nitpick about a team that won the World Series in five games over the Cubs, it would be the A's offense. Despite a lineup that included Hall of Famers Jimmie Foxx (.354, 33 homers, 118 RBIs), Al Simmons (.364, 35 homers, 157 RBIs), and Mickey Cochrane (.331, 7 homers, 95 RBIs), the A's were only third in the majors in runs scored.

The 1906 Cubs—Powerhouses in the regular season with a 116–36 record. Upended in the World Series. Disappointments. The Cubbies did regroup to win titles in 1907 and 1908.

As Thorn discussed comparing teams from different eras, he noted how "Charles Darwin rules baseball," so the 1906 Cubs "wouldn't fare well versus the 1998 Yankees" because players simply improve with time. But, he added, we can "talk about those teams in the same breath because of their measure of dominance" in their era.

I agree with Thorn about the 1906 Cubs having a difficult time against the 1998 Yankees. The Cubs played in the dead ball era, a period where small ball ruled and players tried to chop infield singles and bunted, stole bases, and hit and ran regularly. Home runs were a rarity as the same baseball was often used in the game until it was destroyed. In terms of comparing teams, we can discuss the 1906 Cubs and the 2001 Mariners in the same sentence as the 1998 Yankees because Chicago and Seattle both won a major league best 116 regular season games to New York's 114 wins.

But, when trying to determine the greatest team of all time, it's important to locate the elements that can separate so many outstanding clubs. For me, winning a title is a significant separator. The 1906 Cubs and the 2001 Mariners both led the majors in runs scored per game and in runs allowed per game in their respective seasons. No doubt, that's dominance. However, neither won a championship as the Cubs were shocked by the crosstown White Sox in six games while the Mariners didn't even reach the World Series, losing to the Yankees in five games in the ALCS. I think it's fair to exclude teams from consideration to be called the best of all time because they failed to win a title. We're discussing the best of the best. As we've observed in many Octobers, the team that was number one throughout the six-month regular season can falter during the postseason gauntlet. To me, it's only appropriate to reward the teams who excelled in the marathon of the regular season and also soared in the pressurized sprint of the postseason.

Not everyone agrees with this assessment, including the data crunchers. In 2016, the FiveThirtyEight statistical website calculated the ratings for every major league team in history.

Using the Elo rating, which FiveThirtyEight described as a metric that compares "the relative strengths of teams across the entire history of a league," the website rated the 1906 Cubs as the second-best team in history, despite losing in the World Series. The 1939 Yankees were first, the 1927 Yankees were third, the 1909 Pirates were fourth, and the 1998 Yankees were fifth.

The numbers are the numbers. The ratings are the ratings. The statistics are the statistics. I respect FiveThirtyEight's deep analysis, but I still can't reward a team that ended the season without a championship. Neither can Jeff Nelson, a strong source considering he pitched for the 1998 Yankees and the 2001 Mariners.

"If you're going to be talked about as one of the best of all time, I think you have to finish the deal and win the World Series," Nelson said. "If you look at the 2001 Mariners and the 1998 Yankees, the Yankees were two wins behind in the regular season. But that 1998 team was a much better team."

To Nelson, the differences were the environment and the experience.

"Playing with the Yankees, every game and every series and everywhere we went, it always seemed like a big deal," Nelson said. "And the moment never really got big for us, even though it was the playoffs and the World Series. And you learn how to not let it get bigger than it is because, if you start to do that and let that happen, you're going to fail."

He continued, "I think a lot of guys on the 2001 Mariners, once we got into the postseason, they'd never really had the postseason experience or success. Those guys make the moment bigger than it is and I think that's one of the reasons we didn't go very far."

Jeter agreed about the best team needing to be a championship club.

"I don't say this disrespectfully, but how much do you hear about that Mariners team?" Jeter asked. "You hear about them setting a regular season American League record. But you don't hear about them being amongst the greatest teams ever because they didn't win. You have to win."

I had many conversations with Roger Angell, the graceful baseball writer for the *New Yorker*, in the press box at Yankee Stadium. Angell was kind, smart, and inquisitive, his curiosity for the game never waning. He started writing about baseball in 1962 and had authored an array of brilliant stories, but Angell kept pursuing more answers.

Anyway, I remember how impressed Angell was with the tenacity and the resolve of the Yankees. A couple of weeks after the Yankees had finished squashing everyone in their path and had enjoyed a celebratory parade along the Canyon of Heroes, this is what Angell wrote about them in the *New Yorker*.

"I don't know exactly where these 1998 Yankees come out when compared to the standard all-timers—the 1927 Murderers' Row; the 1961 Mantle-Maris Bronx Bombers; the green-clad Oakland Athletics, who won three consecutive championships in the early seventies; and Cincinnati's Big Red Machine in the middle of that same decade—but I noticed that such arguments are never conclusive and in the end only seem to diminish the flavors and accomplishments of these sublime clubs. In any case, the Yanks' hundred and fourteen regular season victories are second only to the hundred and sixteen of the spitball-era 1906 Chicago Cubs, and their overall hundred and twenty-five wins and fifty losses, or .715, trails the .722 of the 1927 Ruth-Meusel-Combs Yanks, the .747 of those same Cubs (who actually lost the Series that year to the White Sox), and the .717 of the 1909 Pirates. Measuring our Yankees with the everyday yardstick that players and manager use, they wound up 75 games above .500. Unheard of is good enough for me."

As usual, this summation was beautifully written by Angell. Describing what the Yankees did as "unheard of" was, in its own way, putting that team on a pedestal. And, 25 years later, that team, like some other special clubs, remains on a pedestal.

There are valid arguments for a handful of teams being called the best team of all time. History favors the 1927 Yankees. Would any one team truly want to face Ruth and Gehrig in a best of seven series? Run differential favors the 1939 Yankees, who were a lot more than just Joe D. Winning percentage favors the 1906 Cubs, although, again, not winning a title excludes them, for me. Star power favors the 1976 Reds. Eight of their players were All-Stars that season. Depth and balance favors the 1998 Yankees, a team that personified what a team should be.

Twenty-five years ago, Brian Cashman was a first-year general manager who celebrated the glory of shepherding a team that won 125 games. During that season, Don Zimmer, a Yankee bench coach and a baseball lifer, had an impactful conversation with the youthful GM. Wisecracking, but also very wise, Zimmer began his playing career with the Dodgers as Jackie Robinson's teammate in 1954. So Zimmer had experienced a lot of baseball and a lot of baseball history. And he saw what was unfolding with the 1998 Yankees and he made sure to remind Cashman just how remarkable it was.

"Don Zimmer has been in baseball for 50 years and he told me this summer that I'm never going to see another season like this," said Cashman, after the Yankees won it all in 1998. "He was right. If I live to be 100, I'll never see anything like this."

Zimmer was right. We will never see anything like the 1998 Yankees again. A quarter of a century later, no one has matched what that team did. And, until a team does that, the Yankees will stand on top of baseball's mountaintop. The 1998 Yankees can say they were the best team of all time.

"Greatest team ever, greatest team ever, greatest team ever," Jeter once said to me. And then he laughed. But I know he believed it. So do I.

After the Yankees won their 125th game and clinched a World Series title over the San Diego Padres, they celebrated, they rejoiced, and they exhaled. Their long and successful journey to a championship and to a prominent place in baseball history was complete.

But what happened to the players after the 1998 season? Many of the players achieved more glory and won more championships with the Yankees. Many of them also earned more individual accolades. Three of them ended up being voted into the Hall of Fame.

Still, not every post-1998 story involving the Yankee players was sweet and positive. For some players, there were personal and addiction problems. For others, there were criminal and legal issues. And, in the case of Hideki Irabu, there was the ultimate sadness as the pitcher took his own life in 2011.

Across the last 25 years, here are some of the things that the 1998 Yankees have done.

THE 1998 YANKEES

DEREK JETER

Elected into the Baseball Hall of Fame in the Class of 2020 with 99.75% of the vote, the second highest percentage in baseball history.

Accumulated 3,465 hits, the fifth highest total of all time.

Had his number 2 retired and received a plaque in Monument Park in 2017.

Named Yankees' team captain, 2003.

Crested the Turn 2 Foundation.

Helped found the Player's Tribune.

Chief executive officer and part owner of the Miami Marlins, 2017–2022.

MARIANO RIVERA

Unanimously elected into the Baseball Hall of Fame in the Class of 2019. He is the first and only player to ever be unanimously elected.

Compiled 652 saves, the most of all time.

Had his number 42 retired and received a plaque in Monument Park in 2013.

Started the Mariano Rivera Foundation.

Awarded the Presidential Medal of Freedom, 2019.

BERNIE WILLIAMS

Played his final game with the Yankees in 2006. Officially retired in 2015.

Had his number 51 retired and received a plaque in Monument Park in 2015.

What Happened After 1998?

The jazz guitarist has released two albums: 2009's "Moving Forward" and 2003's "The Journey Within."

The 2009 album was nominated for a Latin Grammy.

Received Bachelor of Music from the Manhattan School of Music in 2016.

Director of the National Association of Music Merchants Foundation.

ANDY PETTITTE

Retired after the 2013 season.

Had his number 46 retired and received a plaque in Monument Park in 2015.

High school pitching coach at Houston Second Baptist in 2018.

Pitching coach in Prospect Development Pipeline League, 2019.

Team USA Pitching Coach, 2022–2023.

JORGE POSADA

Retired before the 2012 season.

Had his number 20 retired and received a plaque in Monument Park in 2015.

Marlins' Special Advisor, 2019–2021.

Founded the Jorge Posada Foundation.

PAUL O'NEILL

Retired after the 2001 season.

YES Network broadcaster, 2002–present.

Had his number 21 retired in 2022.

Co-author of *The New York Times* best-seller "Swing and a
  Hit: Nine Innings of What Baseball Taught Me," in 2022.

Received a plaque in Monument Park in 2014.

DAVID CONE

Retired after the 2003 season.

YES Network broadcaster, 2002, 2008, 2011–present.

ESPN broadcaster, 2022–present.

Co-author of *The New York Times* best-seller "Full Count: The
  Education of a Pitcher," in 2019.

Started the David Cone Foundation.

JOE GIRARDI

Retired after the 2003 season.

YES Network broadcaster, 2004.

Yankees' Coach, 2005.

Marlins' Manager, 2006.

FOX Sports broadcaster, 2006.

YES Network broadcaster, 2007.

Yankees' Manager, 2008–2017.

MLB Network broadcaster, 2018–2019.

Philadelphia Phillies' Manager, 2020–2022.

Chicago Cubs broadcaster, 2022–present.

SCOTT BROSIUS

Retired after the 2001 season.

Linfield College Baseball Coach/Assistant Coach, 2002–2015.

Seattle Mariners Triple-A hitting coach, 2016.

What Happened After 1998?

Mariners Assistant hitting coach or third base coach,
2017–2018.

U.S. National Baseball Manager, 2019–2020.

CHUCK KNOBLAUCH

Retired after the 2002 season.

Pleaded guilty to misdemeanor assault of common-law wife
in 2010.

Was charged with assaulting a family member (his ex-wife) in
2014.

Coaches youth players with Trosky baseball in the Houston area.

TINO MARTINEZ

Retired after the 2005 season.

ESPN baseball analyst, 2006.

Special Assistant to the Yankees' General Manager, 2008.

YES Network broadcaster, 2010.

Marlins' hitting coach, 2013.

Team USA hitting coach, 2017.

DARRYL STRAWBERRY

Played his final major league game with the Yankees in 1999.

In May 1999, pleaded no-contest to soliciting sex from a
policewoman posing as a prostitute and for having a small
amount of cocaine. Sentenced to 21 months' probation
and community service.

In September 2000, he rear-ended a car while on painkillers
and tried to drive away. He was arrested and sentenced to
two years of house arrest.

In 2000 and 2001, he twice violated his house arrest and
parole by leaving his drug treatment facility.

In 2002 and 2003, he served 11 months in prison from the
1999 charge.

Authored "Straw: Finding My Way" in 2009.

Inducted into the New York Mets Hall of Fame in 2010.

Born-again Christian evangelist who founded Strawberry
Ministries with his wife, Tracy, in 2011.

Co-authored "The Imperfect Marriage: Help for Those Who
Think It's Over" with Tracy in 2015.

Co-authored "Don't Give Up on Me: Shedding a Light on
Addiction" with Shawn Powell in 2017.

Authored "Turn Your Season Around: How God Transforms
Your Life" in 2021.

TIM RAINES

Elected into the Baseball Hall of Fame in the Class of 2017 on
his 10th and final year of eligibility. Received 86% of the
vote.

Finished with 2,605 hits and 808 stolen bases, the second
highest of all time.

Manager of the Single-A Brevard County Manatees, 2003.

Montreal Expos' coach, 2004.

Chicago White Sox coach, 2004–2006.

Hitting coach for the Harrisburg Senators, 2007.

Manager or Director of Player Development for the Newark
Bears, 2009–2012.

Toronto Blue Jays roving outfield instructor, 2013.

What Happened After 1998?

DAVID WELLS

Co-authored "Perfect I'm Not. Boomer on Beer, Brawls, Back-aches and Baseball" in 2003.

Retired after the 2007 season.

TBS broadcaster, 2009.

FoxSports.com broadcaster, 2011.

Point Loma High School (San Diego) head coach, 2015–2018.

YES Network broadcaster, 2019.

Founded the Perfect 33 Foundation, 2015–present.

ORLANDO "EL DUQUE" HERNÁNDEZ

Retired in 2011.

ESPN Deportes analyst.

SHANE SPENCER

Retired in 2006.

Hitting coach for San Diego Padres' Single-A team, 2008–2012.

Hitting coach for the Somerset Patriots, 2013.

Minor league manager in the Korean Baseball organization, 2016–2019.

Received 70-game ban from KBO for driving under the influence, 2019.

Hitting coach for Saugerties Stallions, 2021.

CHAD CURTIS

Retired after the 2001 season.

In 2013, he was convicted of sexually assaulting three underage female students while working at a high school in Michigan. He served seven years in prison.

Curtis did not respond to multiple interview requests, made
through his lawyer.

CHILI DAVIS

Retired after the 1999 season.

Hitting coach for the Pawtucket Red Sox, 2011.

Oakland Athletics hitting coach, 2012–2014.

Boston Red Sox hitting coach, 2015–2017.

Chicago Cubs hitting coach, 2018.

New York Mets hitting coach, 2019–2021.

JEFF NELSON

Retired in 2007.

MLB.com analyst, 2010.

FOX Sports broadcaster for Marlins, 2016–present.

YES Network broadcaster, 2019–present.

MIKE STANTON

Retired after the 2007 season.

Head coach Don Bosco Prep (NJ), 2010.

MLB Radio Network analyst, 2011.

Houston Astros studio analyst, 2013–present.

RAMIRO MENDOZA

Pitched in his final major league game with the Yankees in
2005.

Pitched for Panama in the 2006, 2009, and 2013 World
Baseball Classic.

Guest instructor at Yankees' Fantasy Camps.

What Happened After 1998?

HIDEKI IRABU

Retired after the 2004 season in Japan, although he returned
and pitched in an independent baseball league in
2009.

In 2008, he was arrested for assaulting a bar manager in
Osaka.

In 2010, he was arrested for driving under the influence in
California.

Irabu was found dead in his home in Los Angeles on July 27,
2011, and it was ruled a suicide by hanging.

GRAEME LLOYD

Retired from professional baseball after the 2003 season.

Pitched for Australia in the 2004 Olympic Games.

Pitching coach for the Perth Heat in the Australian Baseball
League.

HOMER BUSH

Played his final major league game with the Yankees in
2004.

Financial analyst for Merrill Lynch, 2005–2008.

Hitting coach for the Eugene Emeralds, 2014.

Authored "Hitting Low in the Zone: A New Baseball
Paradigm" in 2015.

Texas Rangers, Director of Youth Baseball Programs,
2016.

Manager of the Mahoning Valley Scrappers of the MLB draft
league, 2022.

Manager of Staten Island FerryHawks, 2023.

THE 1998 YANKEES

LUIS SOJO

Initially retired after the 2002 season but returned to play in
2003.

Manager of the Double-A Norwich Navigators in 2002.

Yankees' third base coach, 2004–2005.

Manager of the Single-A Tampa Yankees, 2006–2009 and
2011–2013.

Manager of the Venezuelan National Team in 2006, 2009, and
2013.

Third base coach for Triple-A Scranton/Wilkes-Barre
RailRiders, 2014.

Yankees' Assistant Field Coordinator, 2015.

Manager of Gulf Coast League Yankees, 2017.

Manager of the Spanish National Team, 2019.

DARREN HOLMES

Retired after the 2003 season.

Colorado Rockies bullpen coach, 2015–2019.

Baltimore Orioles assistant pitching coach or bullpen coach,
2020–present.

MIKE BUDDIE

Retired in 2003.

Wake Forest Athletic Administration, 2006–2014.

Furman University Athletic Director, 2015–2019.

United States Military Academy Athletic Director,
2019–present.

What Happened After 1998?

DALE SVEUM

Retired after the 1999 season.

Manager for Double-A Altoona Curve, 2001–2003.

Boston Red Sox third base coach, 2004–2005.

Milwaukee Brewers bench coach or third base coach, 2006–2008.

Brewers Interim manager, September–October 2008.

Brewers hitting coach, 2009–2011.

Chicago Cubs Manager, 2012–2013.

Kansas City Royals Coach and infield instructor, 2013–2014.

Royals hitting coach, 2014–2019.

RICKY LEDÉE

Retired in 2007.

ACKNOWLEDGMENTS

I love baseball. I always have. I love watching it, I love writing about it, and I love talking about it. I feel blessed to have a career in which my life is filled with daily doses of baseball. That means the 10-year-old in me gets to come out and play every day.

As a reporter who has covered major league baseball since 1990, I have seen some superb teams, some good teams, and some awful teams. It's easy to pick the most memorable club I ever covered because it was also the best squad. It was the 1998 Yankees, who I also believe were the greatest of all time.

When Sean Desmond, my editor, suggested writing a 25-year-anniversary book about the vaunted 1998 Yankees, I responded more quickly than it took Mariano Rivera to throw a cutter 60 feet 6 inches. Well, maybe not that fast. But I was beyond enthused to embrace this project and describe the inside story of that historic team.

I want to thank Sean for trusting me with this idea and for all of the passion and care he and his staff showed during this process. David Black, my literary agent, is passionate about books, baseball, and backing his clients. Having both of these true professionals by my side was reassuring.

Acknowledgments

Naturally, this book wouldn't have been as compelling without the cooperation of the 1998 Yankees. Whether it was Joe Torre, Derek Jeter, Bernie Williams, David Cone, Paul O'Neill, Jorge Posada, or so many others, I appreciate their willingness to travel down Memory Lane with me. Twenty-five years later, it was a riveting journey, and I must thank all of the players for sharing their stories, some new, some retold, and all of them intriguing.

As I wrote this book, I received endless support from John J. Filippelli, my boss at the YES Network. He's a boss, but he's also a friend and an excellent resource on Yankees history. I'm grateful to have several YES colleagues who are my friends and who expressed interest in my work. That includes Jared Boshnack, Michael Kay, Bob Lorenz, John Flaherty, David Cone, Meredith Marakovits, Josh Isaac, and Mike Medvin. Researchers Jeff Quagliata and James Smyth were always quick and comprehensive with information. Thanks to Grace Gutierrez, Ray Negron, Marlon Abreu, and Carlos Polanco for their help with translating interviews. Rob, my baseball-loving brother, was a terrific sounding board. I also received support from my sisters-in-law, Suzanne and Tracey; my nephews, Ian, Kyle, and Shane; and my niece-in-law, Caitlin. Courtney Anaya and Lindsey Anaya were the most encouraging cousins.

Having an extra pair of eyes to review a book is invaluable. I had three sets of eyes I could trust, so thank you to Joel Sherman, Greg Gutes, and Chris Garrity for their diligence. Ian O'Connor, Mike Vaccaro, Don Burke, Bob Klapisch, and Sweeny Murti are fantastic journalists who offered advice. Andrew Levy, Kelly Castro, Alex Feuz, Laura Sayers, Steph

Acknowledgments

Panteleakis, Melissa Pena, and the Buonomo family are friends who double as staunch promoters.

As always, I saved the best for last. Pamela, my caring and selfless wife, was a constant source of positivity. She would ask me about my last interview or my latest chapter and would supply smart and timely advice. She was a 24/7 support system, and I couldn't live without her. Thanks for everything, Beanie.

When the final word of the book was written, I closed my laptop and listened to "One Bright Day" by Ziggy Marley. The reasons are self-explanatory. The completion of a book is one bright day and is a reason to celebrate. And 1998 was a year that was filled with a succession of bright days for the best team I've ever seen.

JACK CURRY is an award-winning sports journalist who is an analyst on the Yankees' pregame and postgame shows on the YES Network, where he has worked since 2010. He has won six New York Emmy Awards. Before joining YES, he covered baseball for twenty seasons at the *New York Times*, first as a Yankees beat writer and then as a national baseball correspondent. Curry is also the author of three *New York Times* bestsellers: *Swing and a Hit: Nine Innings of What Baseball Taught Me* with Paul O'Neill, *Full Count: The Education of a Pitcher* with David Cone and *The Life You Imagine* with Derek Jeter. He currently lives in New Jersey.